Gradebusters

How Parents Can End
The Bad Grades Battle

STEPHEN SCHMITZ, PH.D.

bancroft

Published by Bancroft Press ("Books that enlighten")
P.O. Box 65360, Baltimore, MD 21209
800-637-7377
410-764-1967 (fax)
www.bancroftpress.com

ISBN 1-890862-39-8 paper
Library of Congress Control Number: 2004113557

Cover and interior design by Tammy Sneath Grimes
www.tsgcrescent.com, 814.941.7447

---

*To my mother, Evelyn Schmitz, and my mate,
Patricia Walker—good mothers who have moved
on to lead vibrant and fulfilling lives*

CONTENTS

INTRODUCTION   iv

CHAPTER 1   **Are You Fed Up?**   1
             Are You One of Us?   2
             There is a Way Out   5
             Taking Charge   7

CHAPTER 2   **What is School *Really* About?**   10
             Why Kids Get Lost   11
             *What School Is Really About: The Hidden
             Curriculum*   16
             The Culture of Achievement   18

CHAPTER 3   **The Roots of Apathy**   21
             Apathy and Peer Group Conformity   23
             How Apathy Develops   28
             Building Character at Home   38

CHAPTER 4   **Who's in Charge?**   41
             The Dysfunctional Family   47
             Accepting the Responsibilities of Parenthood   54
             *Passive Aggression and the Apathetic
             Underachiever*   55

CHAPTER 5   **Bad Grades and Bad Attitudes**   57
             Tackling the Attitude Problem   59
             This Is Your Problem   68

CHAPTER 6   **Ten Things Parents Do Wrong**   71

CHAPTER 7   **Rights, Responsibilites, and Good Parenting**   90
             Parental Responsibilities and Education   91
             Parents' Rights   93
             Legal Rights and Good Parenting   94
             The Foundations of Good Parenting   97

CHAPTER 8   **School Is a Full-Time Job**   99
             The Policeman Model   99
             A Primer on Payoffs   102
             Bribes, Payments, and Rewards   106

Confronting Your Child About Bad Grades   108
Establishing Natural Consequences   113
Some Suggestions for Consequences   120
The Grace Period   121
Monitoring Your Child's Progress   123

CHAPTER 9   **Getting Down to Business at Home**   126
Reorganizing the Home Front   126

CHAPTER 10   **Forging the Home-School Alliance**   144
When There Is a Problem   150

CHAPTER 11   **The Social Side of School**   155
Fostering a Positive Social Climate   164

CHAPTER 12   **Off to School**   168
Principles of Action   169
The Plan Checklist   171

Elementary School Homework Sheet
Secondary School Homework Sheet

SUMMARY INDEX
ABOUT THE AUTHOR
ABOUT THE BOOK

ACKNOWLEDGEMENTS

I would like to acknowledge the following people: Robert Sherman, Ph.D., and Rodman Webb, Ph.D., two men who instilled in me a passion for education and writing; Bancroft Press's Bruce Bortz, who motivated me to finish this book; the staff of William Lyon School at Orangewood Children's Home, and especially Barbara Blasco, who reminded me of the importance of quality in education; and Patricia Walker, for her suggestions, support, and patience.

I also need to acknowledge the invaluable contributions of the parents I have coached, and my many university students who have taught me more than I taught them. I am truly blessed to have worked with so many individuals who contribute positively to the lives of children.

INTRODUCTION

Self-help books often disappoint the people who buy them. Looking for practical advice and detailed instructions, readers are often introduced to a world of pop psychology, therapeutic introspection, and new-age mysticism, when all they wanted were some simple instructions for fixing a problem. They read on and on, but come away with only vague, flimsy ideas for problem solutions. I have written this book not as a theoretical text, but as a highly practical and usable action plan.

Throughout my years as a counselor and parent trainer, I have been amazed at the degree to which school problems can affect homes and families. Many times, I have dealt with well-meaning parents agonizing over the lethargic school performance of their kids, and fretting endlessly about their child's future career, college, and success. But while participants in my parenting classes often anguished over the bad-grade mess, their children took failure lightly, resenting and complaining about their parents' interference. Tragically, the most responsible parents suffered the greatest, and their homes were filled with arguments, shouting, threats, punishments, and even late night tears, but adolescent attitudes and school grades refused to budge. Finally, parents and I began to share practical ideas about bad grades, and found solutions to the problems surrounding apathetic learners.

I have worked with many sorts of clients: juvenile delinquents, post-incarceration addicts and alcoholics, parents of children with behavioral disorders, abandoned and abused adolescents, disturbed children, teen gangsters, and families of autistic children, among others. Working in educational and therapeutic services is a wonderful and rewarding career. At first, some clients are angry, resentful, and filled with anxiety. Many face seemingly insurmountable emotional and social problems. Others seem downtrodden and despondent, wondering if there is a reason for living. Months later, I see the same clients again, and I feel like I barely know them. Their eyes sparkle. Their speech is filled with merriment and laughter. They tell me about their successes, victories, and blossoming relationships. Their lives are marked with passion and vigor. Life has become interesting and fun again. They seem truly reborn.

There are failures, too. My daughter recently ran into a client, Roland, whom I had met in a recovery center. Jogging in the park one day, she recognized and approached him. Roland was homeless, confused, and sleeping under the bushes. For several days, I searched the same park for him, but to no avail. I contacted the local shelters—also to no avail. His arrival in my daughter's neighborhood park, and his subsequent mysterious disappearance, still haunt me. I wonder what went wrong in Roland's life to cause his relapse into misery.

Counseling is a high stakes business. People come to a therapist because they are unhappy and want to live joyously. Many clients spend miserable years full of anxiety and turmoil. They never realize that the real source of happiness and contentment lies within. It is the therapist's job to tap into that inner source of contentment.

As a beginner, I arrogantly thought that therapeutic successes were the result of my expertise. I blamed myself and felt responsible for failures like Roland. I saw myself as a sort of psycho-mechanic, capable of removing destructive emotions and installing better ones, like a garage mechanic might take out a leaky radiator and put in a new one.

With experience and maturity, I have come to realize that the client does the work and effects the change. Therapists provide guidance, but clients create their own emotional health.

For clients, the work of change is difficult. Yet, they must be willing to produce change if they are to embrace the new, better life they seek. Holding on to old habits, ideas, and values won't work because they are the very mental liabilities that got them into trouble in the first place. Therapists and social workers can often tell which clients are going to make rapid progress because they are the ones who seem ready to accept the necessity of change, regardless of how uncomfortable it may be.

Change is especially difficult for dedicated parents because they are willing to sacrifice and tolerate anything for their kids. It seems ironic, but the most hard-working and idealistic parents are the toughest clients because their notions of good parenting, backed by their passion and dedication, are so inflexible.

Parenting is a hard job for all of us. I believe that there is no right way to parent, because there is no single sort of child. Most parents experience success in some areas of child-rearing, and suffer failure in others. Every child is unique. A struggle with poor grades does not reflect on your parenting skills. You are not struggling alone. Bad grades are a common problem, and they probably are not your fault.

But, you do have the ability to face the facts and decide you are ready to accept change. You *can* put the bad-grade mess behind you and get on with enjoying the better things in life. The beginning lies in recognizing that you have innocently allowed negative habits and ideas to influence your relationships with your kids, and that organizational and attitudinal barriers stand in the way of your children's progress. They must be removed.

My most liberating moment as a parent was when I realized that I needed to change certain things. I did not have the power, or the right, to control my children's development, or to raise them in my own image or likeness. Yet, I could set limits to ensure my own emotional health. I could control my relationships with my children to secure and cultivate my own sense of well-being. Good mental hygiene was my responsibility and my right.

If school grades are causing you stress, anger, and anxiety, isn't it time you took care of yourself, too? You can take charge of your emotional health and cultivate your own sense of well-being as soon as you take charge of your child's education. But, you must accept change if you are to embrace the new, better life that you seek. Haven't you had enough? There is a way out, and the time to find it is now!

CHAPTER ONE

Are You Fed Up?

He who desires, but acts not, breeds pestilence.
—William Blake

The attractive high school freshman in front of me rolled her eyes and groaned plaintively. "You don't understand," she said. "This year, my teachers are *so boring*! They drone on about absolutely nothing for hours, and none of it matters. It's all so stupid and pointless."

This seemingly intelligent adolescent had earned top grades throughout elementary and middle school, but was foundering in her new high school studies. Her mother had brought her to me, complaining that, "All of a sudden, everything about school is totally negative. She doesn't want to go, she doesn't care about her grades, and I can't make her study. She refuses to do anything about her schoolwork and grades, and she won't listen to me when I try to get her back on track. She doesn't care. The school doesn't care. And I am sick and tired of caring when they don't!"

Those of us who face daily battles with a school underachiever know all too well the frustration that comes from nagging, arguing, and constant supervising of our children. The chronic, exhausting cycle of blaming, the excuses for incomplete or inadequate work, the blatant disregard for threats and punishments, and the expressed contempt for anything having to do with school drives many parents to threats, tantrums, feelings of guilt, and expressions of despair. The sense of utter impotence and helplessness about their children's failure is profoundly disheartening. The overt apathy of children and their teachers is both maddening and galling.

◇

Are You One of Us?

Academic underachievement is a problem for the whole family. Responsible parents face exasperating anger, guilt, and resentment because of their baffling inability to solve the "bad grades" dilemma. Students respond to school failure with feelings of frustration and disillusionment. Arguments ensue. Parents blame kids, and kids blame teachers, and teachers blame parents, but nothing happens—nothing changes—and the cycle of underperformance continues unabated. If this sounds like what goes on in your home, ask yourself if your underachieving child seems to fit some of the following patterns:

- ❑ Does your child blame poor scores on boring classes and pedantic, uninteresting teachers?
- ❑ Does your child blame you or others in the family for his or her low performance?
- ❑ Does your child claim to be a victim of incompetent teachers, or teachers who do not like, or carry a grudge, against him or her?
- ❑ Does your child try to sound like a victim of befuddled teachers and inept school administrators?
- ❑ Does your child rationalize poor grades by belittling the value of schooling, saying things like, "It's all just stupid anyhow. I don't learn anything there. It's a complete waste of time."

❑ Does your child, in outright rebellion, refuse to go to school, play hooky, ditch classes, or refuse to do classwork or homework?

❑ Does your child often feign illness on school mornings?

❑ Does your child try to convince you that his or her grades are typical? Does your child say things like, "Everyone in my class is getting grades like mine. The class is really hard."

❑ Does your child claim to be mystified about why his or her grades are so bad?

❑ Does your child insist that he or she doesn't know what to do to bring up his or her grades?

❑ Does your child tell you that he or she is trying as hard as he or she can?

❑ Does your child really not care if he or she does well in school?

❑ Does your child twist discussions about poor grades into arguments about your harsh and unfair parenting?

While you are at it, it might be helpful to take a cold, hard look at yourself and ponder whether you, too, might be stuck in a rut:

❑ Do you sometimes feel like you are trying to motivate someone who has already thrown in the towel?

❑ Do you blame your child's poor grades on a lack of intelligence, "learning problems," special needs or circumstances, poor schools, bad teachers, lack of resources, perceived advantages of the other kids, teacher biases, favoritism, or the excuse that a teacher is boring or "doesn't like" your child?

❑ Do you buy into your kid's blaming and excuses for lackluster performance?

Gradebusters

- ❏ Do you perceive low marks as a systemic failure, brought about by the abysmal performance of our nation's schools, falling standardized test scores, teacher shortages, scarce budget resources, overfilled classes, unprepared faculty, and the politicizing of classroom instruction?
- ❏ Do you recount the "good old days" when you were in school and things were better?
- ❏ Do you find yourself arguing, shouting, and issuing threats about school and grades?
- ❏ Do you spout old adages like, "Boys will be boys!" or "You can lead a horse to water, but you can't make him drink," to try to minimize the gravity of your child's poor grades?
- ❏ Do you go to the school and take your child's side against the school's teachers and administrators, blaming them for your youngster's behavior or performance?
- ❏ Do you feel powerless to effectively intervene to stop the deteriorating school performance of your kids?
- ❏ Do you take personally your child's poor scores and your arguments about them?
- ❏ Do you become angry and resentful?
- ❏ Do you quit confronting your youngster entirely about bad grades in order to keep peace at home?

If the patterns of behavior revealed by these questions sound familiar, you are probably beyond frustration. You have changed tactics. You have waited hopefully for a new teacher, school, or academic year to turn things around. You have rationalized that your underachiever is just going through a "phase."

In fact, you have tried just about everything, and nothing seems to help. The teacher has little to offer in the way of suggestions or assistance. Your child is struggling and getting nowhere, or even worse, is obviously not trying at all and does not care if you know it. Nagging your child seems to trigger anger and sullenness, but no improvement. You are at your wit's end. You are fed up with your child, the teacher, the school, and the whole mess!

◈

There is a Way Out

If you are feeling fed up for the last time, if you are ready for real change, then this book is for you. It is a set of simple directions designed to change the school performance of your child for the better—academically, behaviorally, and socially.

Necessarily, your attitudes about children and schooling, and how you manage and discipline your youngster, will have to change. This book may ask you to do things that will make you uncomfortable. You will have to examine many aspects of your child's education, and even your child's teachers, from a new perspective. You will be called upon to accept new responsibilities that you may not want, or that you believe should be the job of others. You are going to have to learn to say, "No!" and mean it.

But, there is a way out, if you are really, finally, fed up with excuses, blaming, moping, guilt, and anxiety about the school grades mess, if you are willing to take certain steps, make certain sacrifices, and, finally, take charge of your child's education and your own sanity. Once you admit to yourself that you have finally had it, that you are sick and tired of rotten grades and ready for a change, substantial progress may be easier than you think.

Whatever you might be thinking at this stage of the game, one thing is for certain. Whatever you are doing now is not working. If you are genuinely fed up, then you should be willing to try something else. What do you have to lose by considering some new ideas about yourself, your child, and the school involved in your child's education?

Perhaps the most important principle of this book—a notion you must take to heart first and foremost if you really want to improve the school quandary you find yourself in—is:

If nothing changes, nothing changes.

You cannot continue to do the same things and expect different results. The same old nonsense just isn't going to work.

I have a dear friend, Barbara, a young professional who is an avid reader of self-help books. Doctors John Gray, Phil McGraw, and Richard Carlson—in her extensive library she has the complete collections of these celebrated authors, and many more besides. She is a cornucopia of popular diet information, new age philosophy, and ideas about the latest guru, and is always on the lookout for a better means of self-analysis or a new path to enlightenment.

Although she reads the books, she does not seem to change. Her attitudes, beliefs, values, and behaviors remain the same. She fails to see that the simple act of reading these books does not provide a remedy—the books can only improve her life if she actually takes the suggestions detailed in them and applies them to her daily life. She is engrossed in the abstract world of ideas, but change takes place in the here and now.

Buying and reading this book will be a waste of time unless you decide to take its suggestions to heart and apply them to your interactions with your son or daughter, their teachers, and the administrators of the school they attend. Reading this book will be useless unless you incorporate its suggestions into your ideas, beliefs, and opinions.

Change is uncomfortable and a lot of work. In the process of changing, you may have to accept some ugly truths about yourself and your child. Yet, if you have had enough of the excuses and apathy, and are ready to accept anything, even change, to finally get results at school, then read on.

◇

Taking Charge

This book is about taking charge of your child's education. It is not a book about the plight of our nation's schools. Discussions of the latest educational research, national education policy, teacher training, psychology, and learning theories have all been cut to a minimum. Avoided altogether are lengthy discussions of facts and statistics. This book focuses solely on the strategies you need to employ and the actions you need to take to get your child back on track at school.

Nor is this book an academic text or a publication for professionals, although teachers may well find it useful and worthwhile. It is not about ADD/ADHD, Dyslexia, ED/EH, Developmental Disabilities, Special Education, or education of the severely disadvantaged. These kinds of learning problems are important and valid, and the bookstores are full of special books about these special problems.

This book is for other kinds of underachievers: lounge lizards too lazy to study; computer geeks who would rather surf the net than do their homework; athletes and cheerleaders who feel they have already "made it" in school; smart kids who see themselves as too brilliant to bother with mundane lessons—and many others who don't fit these admittedly stereotypical, but real-life, types of kids. This book directly attacks the problem of kids who are not making it in school because their attitudes are getting in the way of their success.

Brad was a 10th grader whom I met when I was recruited as a consultant on his case. He had been placed in an alternative education program within a residential treatment center for behavioral disorders. His parents complained that Brad refused to follow home rules and parental instructions, played hooky from school, and was belligerent to teachers. Brad apparently refused to take all directions from parents, teachers, and other adults and spent most of his time as a recluse, isolated in front of his computer.

When I spoke to Brad, he freely admitted ignoring schoolwork and refusing to follow the directions of his adult caregivers. "I learn from computers," he said matter-of-factly, "because school is not a challenge for me. I am super intelligent, and I really think I am too smart to waste my time in a school run for average kids. I have a genius I.Q., and I belong to MENSA, an organization for geniuses. I don't think the teachers are as smart as I am; I know my parents aren't. I have already mastered C++ and HTML, and I could probably find a good job anytime I wanted to. I think the kids at school are children. I have my own friends through the net. I can't think of one good reason I should waste my time with a high school education. So, I just don't go."

It is important to note that Brad's problems were not what we traditionally term "learning problems." Brad had an *attitude* problem. His skewed beliefs about himself and his entitlements, and his apathetic outlook toward traditional education, were getting in the way of his progress in school.

This book is designed as a field guide for frustrated parents whose children have all sorts of attitude problems. It encourages parents to manage their children's lives in different ways. But it is really a "self-help" book because its purpose is to help parents overcome exasperation and bring peace into their households by winning the home-school battle. It is written for lay parents whose children are not achieving at school, and for parents who are seeking concrete strategies that will point themselves and their children in different, more academically productive directions. It explains in detail how to get children back on the road to achievement at school. It is a book for parents who want and need to take charge of their child's education.

CHAPTER TWO

What is School Really About?

In the first place, God made idiots. This was for practice.
Then he made school boards.
—Mark Twain

How long has it been since you balanced a chemical equation? How many times during the typical week do you diagram a sentence? Do you remember the difference between a phrase and a clause?

We all learned this information in school (or should have), but most academic information fails to follow us from the schoolhouse into our adult lives. Much of the inert, seemingly trivial knowledge we learn in school is quickly forgotten. We seldom remember more than a fraction of the facts we memorize for our tests and teachers. So, as our kids ask all the time, "What's the point?"

At first glance, our child's complaints about teachers who "drone on for hours . . . and none of it matters one bit" might seem valid. But such accusations are unfounded and dangerous. Important things go on at school. If your child is not thriving in the school environment, your child is losing out. Your child is missing out on the facts and figures presented in class. But a more critical loss is your child's lack of involvement in the school's culture of achievement.

Why Kids Get Lost

It is indisputable that our public schools are in a crisis. *Why* they are in a crisis is a matter of some contention. Every school probably has its share of lazy, incompetent, or burned out teachers, and some schools are undeniably better than others. Yet, blaming the school or the teacher for your child's underperformance has one serious drawback—it does not help your child succeed.

Many of the schools' problems are systemic, meaning your child's performance at school may be affected by problems within the modern school bureaucracy as a whole. However, this book is not about the bureaucracy of education. It is about the bureaucracy of the home. Yet, a few systemic problems deserve mention simply because you must understand these issues in order to help your child rise above them.

Classrooms are overcrowded. I recently visited a core city middle school in California's Long Beach Unified School District. The principal pointed out that every school classroom was filled to the maximum of 30 students set by school board policy, and that each teacher taught six such groups daily.

Citing budget problems, neighboring Tustin city schools recently revoked a 20-student limit on class size at the lowest grade levels.

Incredibly, upper level classes in our nation's poorest school districts can contain as many as 50 students, and under national "mainstreaming" guidelines, some of these students may have severe emotional, behavioral, or learning problems.

Frankly, most teachers' classroom time is spent dealing with the students who have the severest problems. Often, there is little time left over for the others in the class.

Teachers feel as if they are under the gun. This is the age of school accountability. School testing, district testing, and state and national standards dominate curricula and instructional programs. Nowadays, evaluators, assessors, auditors, curriculum coordinators, special education teachers, and parents all feel they have the right to question what educators do—to evaluate the effectiveness of classroom instruction, and to intrude upon classrooms that used to be the sacrosanct territory of the teacher.

Meantime, classroom teachers seldom have free time for planning and developing new strategies. Their days are filled with conferences, visits, assessment reports, achievement tests, special education planning and progress meetings, and program modernization seminars.

I often work with California's Orange County ACCESS program at a local community shelter school. Students at this school have been removed from their homes because of alleged abuse, neglect, or parental criminality. Many of the students are severely traumatized. Most are years behind grade level. A teacher at the school told me that although her students were often disruptive, inattentive, under-prepared, and at-risk, she had it easier than other teachers in the district because, "at least I don't have to deal with any parents." With all the new issues of accountability and programming, she said, she was surprised that normal teachers could get any teaching done at all!

Teachers may not have it as bad as they think they do, but that is not the point. Teachers feel as if they are under the gun and that everyone is examining and questioning their standards, competence, and efficacy. For some teachers under pressure, parents who want answers and solutions to their children's academic failure seem like an additional burden, an imposition from a group they see as adversarial, hostile, and often threatening.

In the American education system, everyone thinks they're an expert. In Japan, France, Russia, or Brazil, a national ministry comprised of experts in educational administration, curriculum coordination, and learning psychology runs the schools. There are national standards based on a national curriculum and nationally approved texts.

In America, by contrast, schools are run by literally thousands of locally administered school boards composed of lawyers, plumbers, real estate agents, and housewives who decide everything from who shall learn what and when, to how the schools should be funded and what textbooks should be adopted. In our democratic way of thinking, each of us should have a voice in the education of our children.

Added to this problem is the voter mentality that everyone should have a voice in school decision-making. Most citizens would never dream of demanding a voting partnership in the administration of their community's hospitals, power plants, police stations, or prison systems. Yet, voters expect schools to be open to public access, public scrutiny, and public decision making, effectuated through a local school board of peers selected from the community by local vote.

Somehow, everyone assumes that their own experience in the public schools makes them qualified to make decisions about how schools should be funded and operated. Populism and politics, economics and special interests, pop psychology, and TV programming often win out in decision-making, while educational research, professional expertise, and expert opinion are frequently ignored.

Although the democratic mentality of shared decision-making in public education is progressive and laudable, the end result is often a disorganized hodgepodge of conflicting rules and procedures. Students who move from one district to another may find themselves using a different textbook, taking different subjects, or being placed at entirely different levels at the new school. Often, districts adopt policies based on special interests, local politics, and local economics, or even on who shows up at the school board meetings.

Parents operate under the assumption that somewhere, somehow, scientific experts are involved in the operation of their schools' programs and oversight, when the cold fact is that your particular school district may be administered by a group of individuals whose expertise and credentials are marginal at best.

Our schools' clients have changed. Years ago, students concerned themselves with dating, grades, managing jobs and homework, getting to school on time, and being ready for class. Today, schools are a place of dedicated police units, metal detectors and security procedures, drug deals and gang warfare, open sexuality and promiscuity, isolation, fear, and violence. Student problems are compounded by the dissolution of the traditional core family, minimal child supervision in overworked single-parent homes, and increased poverty among school-aged core city children.

Fewer parents are able and willing to actively help their children with their classwork or homework. Personal emergencies, family crises, peer relationships, and issues involving the negative impact of drugs, sex, and violence often dominate the lives of our school-aged children.

Increasingly, the schools have been required to intervene in non-academic issues and offer educational and social programs to help alleviate modern social ills. While national standards and state norms mandate increasingly rigid academic standards, a growing portion of the teaching day is spent distributing anti-smoking information, discussing HIV awareness, demonstrating how to use condoms, staging DARE assemblies, conducting "Just Say No" campaigns, and practicing emergency security procedures in case a gunman or terrorist shows up on or near school grounds.

Add together the ruckus surrounding school administration and accountability, educational special interest groups competing in a political environment, teachers facing increased accountability in packed, unruly classrooms, and classes full of students operating under tremendous pressure from a variety of modern problems, and the end result is that many kids get lost in the shuffle. Your child may not be getting the attention he or she needs in order to thrive in the classroom.

Callous as it may sound, schools increasingly offer a mass-produced product suitable for some children. At the same time, many kids in academic trouble are left to their own devices, to cope and adapt if they can, or to fall into the quagmire of mediocrity, underachievement, and failure if they can't. Intervention is often available for certain special education students with specifically identifiable disabilities, but schools have few resources to offer students who are simply struggling with assignments and grades. Schools seem to have adopted a "right to fail" policy for the kids who are apathetic and lazy, or have other attitude problems, but these kids need an education, too.

If your child is faring poorly at school, there is a chance that he or she may not get the fundamental academic preparation necessary for a future career. A more fundamental danger, however, is that your child may miss the necessary education about the culture of achievement that enhances life chances and makes future success a possibility.

What School is Really About: The Hidden Curriculum

Schools are the great socializing agents of our culture, and successful students have learned the great lesson of education's "hidden curriculum." Our schools teach future citizens how to contribute to, and prosper within, our society. The school experience instructs children in a multitude of attitudes, skills, and behaviors they will need if they expect to thrive in the modern workforce—everything from arriving on time, doing work accurately, paying attention to quality, and following directions.

School introduces future citizens to the culture of achievement—the expectations and values demanded of successful citizens in our society. If your child is not performing well at school, for whatever reason, chances are that he or she has not experienced and accepted the culture of achievement, has not learned its lessons, or has not bought into its values.

For many years, I trained prospective teachers on the American mainland and abroad. In one of my most useful exercises for my future educators, I asked them to list the most important aspects of their prospective job. The exercise read something like this:

✦

Imagine in the future that you are recruited by a revolutionary new school district. In this district, instead of twelve years of public school instruction, each student is allowed only one full day of education, offered by an expert teacher who meets with the student to impart the most important knowledge and distilled wisdom of our culture and society.

You have been hired to be one of these teachers. You must prepare for one day of instruction, the only and most important education your student will ever receive. What will you teach?

Most teaching novices seemed startled and perplexed by the assignment, but soon got to work. Many lists included a love of learning, an appreciation of beauty, and a respect for others. My students aspired to teach their young charges to love life. They wanted their students to understand the value of hard work and the centrality of family. Several future teachers mentioned the importance of ethics and morality.

No one listed a class in the Periodic Chart of Elements or the grammar of diphthongs. My student teachers did not think that facts—like how to balance chemical equations—were very important.

School, you see, is not just about learning facts and figures, mathematics, history, or how to balance chemical equations. The most important lessons to be gained in school will not be found in any curriculum. School is about attitudes. School is about learning to be successful. School is about putting in the work to get the results you want. School is about investing in your future today to reap rewards tomorrow. School is about respecting others, working with others, accepting direction from others, accomplishing mutual goals, and learning to do a job well. School is about all the things that help us become happy and successful adults in our society.

The Culture of Achievement

One reason children are missing out on the culture of achievement is that the values and expectations of youth have changed so drastically.

I once had a counseling session with a troubled fifteen-year-old student named Jamie. She had been sent to our behavioral facility by her parents because of her frequent truancy, chronic drug use, overt sexual activity, and outright rebellion against her parents' rules and values.

I asked Jamie about her career goals, and she explained to me that she wanted to enter medical school and become a neurosurgeon. She noted that neurosurgery seemed like a good career choice because "I want to make a lot of money. I want to have an important job where I am a somebody and I can help people out. I want to have money to help my family and parents."

I pointed out to Jamie that her career plans entailed a great deal of work and study, and that such laudable aspirations did not match her present attitudes and lifestyle. Strangely, Jamie saw no inconsistency between her present behavior and her future goals. She scoffed at the notion that her behavior today might influence her chances of success tomorrow. As she explained, "Being a doctor has nothing to do with that stuff. You just don't think I can do it."

For Jamie, career success was a product of simply wanting something, feeling entitled to it, and then expecting it to become a reality. In my counseling and education experience, I often encounter this sense of entitlement. I believe it has become a common theme for a large portion of our youth. In a twisted sort of logic, adolescents believe that if they want something, and others seem to have it, then the world will automatically provide it to them.

❈

In a discussion with me, Melanie, age 23, single, and a customer service representative, vented her frustration about her lack of career advancement and material success. Although she had performed abysmally through three years of high school and then dropped out before graduating, she observed that, "There are all kinds of people out there my age who are already millionaires. They already own big companies. I don't even have a good job. I expected to have been really successful by now. It's depressing. It's just not fair."

Jamie and Melanie fail to see a connection between hard work, deferred gratification, and success in life. Entirely missing is the notion that dedication drives achievement. They view success as a given—either a right or a stroke of luck that they are entitled to by virtue of the fact that they want it.

Schools, on the other hand, teach a different lesson. Academically successful students earn their success through an investment of time, energy, and hard work. They get things done. They follow directions. Good students apply themselves to reach goals. They accept a structure of authority and work within it. They earn their rewards instead of simply expecting them. They are involved in a culture of achievement. And, the important values they learn follow these achievers into and throughout adulthood.

If your child is not "getting it" in school, he is probably not "getting" these important lessons, either. And, although the school and teacher may want to help, they may not have the resources, time, or expertise to spare. You are probably going to have to provide any and all help yourself, because nobody else will. You are going to have to take charge of your child's education.

CHAPTER THREE

The Roots of Apathy

I am not young enough to know everything.
—Oscar Wilde

Parents who face apathetic learners may look back at the roots of their child's listless attitude about school and learning, and wonder where they went wrong. The first few years of school, it seems, were exciting—even a bit scary—but generally successful. Their child settled into some comfortable routines, and things went smoothly for awhile. But somewhere, often in the middle grades, things began to go awry. Negative comments about school and teachers seeped into conversations. Homework became a burden and started to cause daily conflicts. Grades dropped. The child avoided parents' questions about falling grades, or met inquiries with anger and resentment. Somewhere, somehow, something went seriously wrong. Parents wonder, "How did it happen?"

Corey loved to go to her kindergarten class near her mother's workplace at the university. After school, she eagerly waited to be picked up so that she could tell her amused mother all about the exciting things that had happened at school, and show off the crafts she had made. Dinnertime discussions focused on school poems, good books, and the latest kindergarten gossip. Corey's

21

parents conscientiously read to her nightly, and were impressed when she began to read passages along with them. Corey's teacher, a polished university intern, assured the parents that Corey was bright, involved, and developmentally advanced. Mom and Dad were thrilled!

The transition into public school seemed to go well, too, although Corey sometimes felt overwhelmed by the large school, older children, and the size of her class. She reported a few conflicts with peers, and complained that her teacher was a bit boring. The enthusiasm of the nightly dinner table discussions slacked off, but Corey's parents were not concerned. After all, Corey was a good student with a strong intellect and solid student skills. She was doing fine.

By fifth grade, however, things had become more serious and Corey's parents realized there was a problem. Progress notes arrived from the school indicating that Corey had not turned in work, that assignments were incomplete or of poor quality, and that she was not participating in class. Many of her report card grades were "U"—unsatisfactory. At the parent-teacher conference Corey's mother arranged, the teacher explained that Corey was behind her peers academically and socially, was passive and disinterested in class, and seldom turned in complete assignments. According to the teacher, "Corey has the ability, but she just doesn't seem to care. And I can't make her learn if she won't try."

I met Corey when she was in the 8th grade. Her parents had brought her in for a psychological evaluation at our behavioral clinic. By then, Corey's attitude had further deteriorated along with her grades. Her parents wanted an assessment to find out if there was a psychological disorder underlying her academic and social problems. After a complete assessment, I assured them that Corey had no identifiable clinical disorder.

Strangely, they seemed disappointed by the diagnosis. They

were seeking an answer for what they hoped was a malady. They wanted a remedy and a quick fix, but all I had to offer was a partial explanation for her apathy towards school, and some solid parental advice.

I explained to Corey's family that apathy is not an identifiable illness. It is not caused by a specific disorder, and is not curable by a simple remedy. Apathy develops over time, usually because of a combination of interrelated causes. In children, some of the roots of apathy involve specific incidents that shape attitudes. Other factors are developmental, and involve the growth of the child's independent social relationships.

◇

Apathy and Peer Group Conformity

In early childhood, a youngster's main social relationships involve the home, family, and siblings. Most information comes from Mom and Dad, who also teach home values, beliefs, and rules for behavior. Important emotional bonds form around the home and family. This "nuclear family" is the center of the young child's intellectual, social, and emotional life.

When children begin school, however, their circle of social relationships broadens. The teacher enters the picture as another adult with authority, influence, and information. This new, powerful adult may seem distant and frightening. The social rules the child follows for grown-ups may not work with the teacher. New expectations must be met. And, although parental love and attention are unconditional, the teacher's attention and approval may be conditional on hard work, good grades, and proper behavior based on new and difficult criteria.

Homebound children see their parents as experts in all things. Yet, at school, the new teacher may present information different from what the child has accepted as the unquestioned truths of the parents. Established ideas and values are brought into question. I quit smoking after 25 years when my youngest daughter came home from kindergarten one day and announced, "Daddy, my teacher says that smoking is stupid and will kill you. Why do you smoke if it is stupid? Is it going to kill you?" My parental authority was no longer absolute. My child was beginning to see that the world is full of opinions, and that her parents' beliefs and values are open to question.

Another social event occurs during the early school years that has a direct impact on a child's perspective. At school, children begin to develop long-term peer relationships. Friends supercede the home and parents as the focus of the child's social life. Soon, kids prefer friendships to home relationships and spend more time with peers than parents. By the onset of adolescence, teens see their friends as their most important source of information.

Their peers also become their primary source of status, validation, companionship, and comfort. Ideas, beliefs, and values emerge that are peer-centered instead of home-taught. Kids turn to the styles, mannerisms, music, habits, and behaviors common among their friends. In many instances, kids abandon the values they learned at home, and those of the peer group become paramount.

✿

Jan's mother was at wit's end. Jan had been a seemingly "normal" girl in junior high school. Then, in high school, she met new friends and, according to her mother, "bad things" began to happen. Jan began to wear more provocative clothing. She seldom came home before curfew, and she usually went out with older boys. She had her tongue pierced, and, her mother found out later, her nipples, too. Jan and her friends began to use coarse language around her home, and mocked her parents' religious beliefs and traditional values.

Things came to a head when Jan asked her mother to take her to a clinic for birth control pills. The mother, aghast, refused, demanding to know why Jan would need a contraceptive. Jan countered that she had been sexually active for some time, with several different boys, and did not want to become pregnant. But, Jan added, she was not about to give up sex or any of the other things she and her friends were doing.

"Look, Mom," Jan explained. "We all have sex. Kids do that at my school. Things are different now. We drink, we get high, and we have sex. We party. I know that you think that is wrong, but we don't think so. If I acted like you, my friends would think I was weird. I'm not doing anything wrong, and I don't care if you disagree."

An odd sort of contradiction develops during adolescence. Youngsters try to demonstrate their emerging independence and "coolness" by adopting counterculture fashions and tastes. Kids use dyed hair, raggedy pants, spiked clothes, or tattoos as statements that they are independent from the tastes and values of their parents, and have adopted the values of their "own" social group. The contradiction arises because teens often do not see their lack of independence—they are merely conforming to a different set of values. They adhere to the values of their peers more slavishly than they ever conformed to their parents' wishes.

In Jan's case, her friends' influence had become so powerful that the values of her home and family became meaningless. She believed that her new lifestyle was typical of kids her age, but it isn't. Sexual promiscuity and substance abuse may seem more commonplace today, but they are not the norm and they do not need to be accepted.

Jan's problem arose not only because she was a conformist, but also because she was conforming to the values of an extremely undesirable peer group. Her friends openly engaged in behaviors that were unacceptable at home, and Jan decided that if these things were OK for her friends, they were OK for her, too. Not surprisingly, Jan's peers thought that school was not for them. When Jan's friends began to drop out, she did too.

After transferring to a new high school, Jan's grades took a nosedive. A few months after approaching her mother about birth control pills, Jan announced to her parents that she was dropping out of school on her 16th birthday, the youngest age permitted in her state. She claimed that school had no future value for her, that most of her friends had already left school, and that there would be nothing there for her. Jan explained her school apathy, and her decision to drop out, by claiming, "I want to get married soon, and [my boyfriend] Buddy will take care of me. I want to be a bartender as soon as I'm old enough. I want to get a job and save up some money. My friends all have apartments. I can stay with them until I get my own. I don't know much from school, but I'm street smart, and know how to take care of myself."

Jan had some specific complaints about school, too. "I don't care about school. I don't like the people there, and they don't like me. The teachers all think they can boss people around. I'm always in trouble there. I don't think those people should tell me what to wear or what to do. I can take care of myself. All my friends dropped out, and they're doing fine. They do what they want and they're having fun. I hate school. Those people at school really piss me off!"

Hidden within Jan's angry statements are some interesting revelations. Did you notice how often she referred to her friends? Did you see how she seemed to compare her peers to "those people," as if her friends were knowledgeable insiders and everyone else were nameless outsiders who knew nothing? Jan described her new values as what "we" believe. She insisted that education was worthless because all her friends had dropped out—and it must be a smart choice because they made it. She was angry at imagined injustices at school. Jan wanted to bypass the inconvenience of school and get on with what should come afterwards—marriage, career, and family. She was looking for a shortcut to adulthood.

We will continue Jan's story later, but for now, it is important to clarify the part her peers played in her apathy towards education. They convinced her that her home values were irrelevant to a modern, "progressive" lifestyle. They demonstrated, to her satisfaction, that school was not important or valuable. They encouraged her to try prohibited behavior, like alcohol and sex, against her parents' wishes. They suggested that she could thrive without education. They acted as if adulthood was a choice, not a process, and that Jan could commence being an adult any time she wanted.

Apathy springs from a wide range of attitudes and beliefs about life and success. Family values and upbringing play a part, as does a youngster's self-image. But peer pressure often is *the* determining factor. In Jan's case, apathy about school grew out of the negative attitudes of her friends about the value of education. It was easy for Jan to become apathetic when her friends felt the same way. To them, dropping out was "cool."

How Apathy Develops

Your child's apathy probably did not arise from one specific source, but developed over time from several antecedents. Apathy about school can originate from a variety of sources besides the pressures of social conformity.

Some common precursors of school apathy include:

Exaggerated self-image. Young people seem to admire all the wrong characteristics in themselves and others. Group status, rebelliousness, physical attractiveness, athleticism, and daring often lead to social success in school. Some children assume that these traits will make them successful as adults, too. After all, these things have worked well so far, haven't they?

When youngsters are socially successful without academics, it is difficult for many of them to see that, in the future, the rules of success will change. Some adolescents come to believe there is no payoff in education—they are doing fine without it, and what has made them so successful right now will continue to make them successful in the adult world.

Unreasonable expectations and future goals. A similar problem often arises among young people who are talented and rely on these talents exclusively for their future success. Athletes, singers, musicians, and writers may assume that their abilities in a certain area will define their career success.

✦

Lashawn was a slender, attractive African-American sixteen-year-old who I worked with at a county shelter school. Pretty, outgoing, and athletic, she had her choice of friends and suitors. She enjoyed basketball, and we often played a pick-up game together while we chatted about her life and her future.

Lashawn freely admitted to me that she loved the social side of school, but spurned its academic side. She aspired to play basketball professionally, and, according to Lashawn, studying would do her no good on the professional basketball court.

Lashawn had read somewhere that the NWBA drafted talented players directly out of high school, and nothing I could say could detach her from the notion that she would leave high school for a promising career in women's professional basketball. I told her frankly that she wasn't that good. I explained that NWBA players are typically drafted out of colleges. I pointed out that if things didn't work out in basketball, Lashawn needed a backup plan. I encouraged her to hope for the best but to plan for the worst.

Lashawn countered that she was successful in everything she did. She had friends and supporters. Boys found her fascinating. "I may not be good at the books," she said, "but I know how to take care of myself and make things happen. I'm good and I know it. I don't need to sit in a classroom and learn stuff I don't like."

Lashawn fell into both of the preceding apathy traps. She had an exaggerated view of her talents, brought on by her social success at school. She had the unreasonable expectation of being discovered by a national scout at a children's shelter. Tragically, her popularity and outspoken opinions about the lack of value in academics were infectious. Many of her friends, peers, and admirers took her opinions to heart, and they also became disinterested in school.

Gradebusters

Frustration and projected anger. For many young people, the academics, class rules, and social competition of school are frustrating and a bit frightening. Youngsters are acutely aware of their status and social standing at school, and try hard to impress their peers. Teachers-in-training are instructed to never belittle children in front of the class because children dread such public embarrassment. Unfortunately, some teachers do mock their students. Public schools can be cruelly impersonal. Peers can become bullies and teasers. Youngsters often ridicule others in an attempt to bolster their own status.

As a result, many children view school as a place of embarrassment and shame. When school is viewed as a source of social discomfort, it is hard not to become frustrated and angry. Some students try to punish the school and its teachers by withdrawing from classwork and refusing to participate. They fail to see how this passive aggression is destructive of their own future success.

⌗

I taught Bao in a gifted and talented 4th grade class in Southern California. The son of Vietnamese immigrants, Bao was a smart and competitive student who struggled to be the very best at all things academic. I often complimented him on his academic astuteness, and it was clear that he relished the praise and attention.

One day, Bao turned in a two-day math assignment, and the majority of his answers were wrong. I noticed that he was consistently making the same sort of error in his calculations. I pointed out the error, showed him a few problems done correctly on the board, and asked him to redo the assignment. One look at Bao, and I knew he was furious! I asked him why he seemed angry, and he threw his books against the wall and stormed out of the room.

When he returned to class, Bao simply sat and read, refusing to do his class assignments. "I don't care anymore!" he shouted when I asked him about his missing work. "Just leave me alone!"

What had I done to so anger and alienate this bright youngster? Later, I called his mother, who suggested that he felt humiliated because I had put the correctly done problems on the board, where he perceived that everyone could view his failings. He believed he had lost status, and refused to participate in class further.

Bao was frustrated because he answered the problems incorrectly. His frustration turned into anger when he felt criticized and believed he had lost face with his peers.

Enabling parents. Parents may enable their children to become apathetic when they ignore budding problems, try to protect children from the consequences of their actions, help excessively with schoolwork and homework, or place the blame for academic shortcomings on themselves, others, or circumstances. Youngsters learn that they can be lazy and can avoid taking responsibility for their grades. After all, why should they bother to be responsible? Their parents always rationalize their behavior and then bail them out!

Do you remember Jan, the aspiring drop-out at the beginning of the chapter? Her parents went to the school and confronted the principal, blaming him and everyone else because Jan was apathetic towards school and wanted to quit. Jan's father confided to me that he had gone to the school expressly to complain and to set the school straight. He bragged to me about how he had told the principal off. He said to the principal that:

Gradebusters

"I understand why Jan is doing so badly here. She doesn't like the classes and she doesn't like the school. I don't know how kids can take school seriously when the classes and teachers are so awful. Nobody gave her help when her grades started to fall, and no one told me when she started to have problems. You people don't teach much of anything that interests her, and it's hard to make her come to school when she thinks it's so boring. You want me to do something about it, but you aren't doing anything to help my daughter out.

"Jan hates this place, and I don't like it much, either. The other kids don't like her, and she doesn't get along with them. She gets into fights, and no one tries to help her or keep the other kids from picking on her. This school is full of snotty cliques. The girls all snub her. And Jan hates to come and get made fun of.

"You people don't want kids to drop-out, but you don't do much to help girls like Jan out. You make school hard to like. The classes are too hard and really boring, and then everyone picks on her. Hell, if I was her age, I think I'd want to drop out, too."

I worked closely with the school on a daily basis, and there were several grains of truth to his accusations. Jan's father did several things right when he confronted the school's principal. He arranged a meeting, voiced his concerns honestly, and made the principal responsible for the social welfare of his child.

But he blundered when he became rude. His anger, aggressive tactics, blaming, and failure to propose a plan of action diminished his credibility. He had known about Jan's problems for months, but put off going to school until it was too late. He placed blame for Jan's deteriorating academic performance and apathetic attitude directly on the school, essentially letting Jan, and himself, off the hook.

Fear and avoidance. When Jan's father complained about the social situation at her school, one point rang true. For some students, school has always been a place of snobbery and social cruelty. Today, many children fear going to school. Public schools are more violent than ever before, and the best academic schools are often as dangerous as the worst. Campus security officers, metal detectors, locker checks, and urine drug testing are common. Alcohol and illicit drugs are sold on playgrounds and in halls. Kids get high in school parking lots. With the social pressures and open delinquency present at some schools, public education can be an intimidating and frightening proposition. Anxiety and stress can cause listless participation and withdrawal. Apathy is an escape from a social scene some kids find brutal.

Rebelliousness and laziness. When kids become angry and rebellious, what better way to strike out against authority than to rebel against education and school? Demonstrating apathy against learning allows youngsters to challenge the authority of the home and the institutions of their society. At the same time, they can conveniently avoid a great deal of hard work. "Avant-garde" or "new age" youths may denounce the worthlessness of education, thereby creating an excuse for abandoning their studies and creating free time for other, more leisurely and pleasurable pursuits.

Gradebusters

✧

Cindy was a quiet sixteen-year-old drop-out who was admitted to our residential treatment program for depression and drug dependence. She had dyed her hair jet black. She wore only black clothing and dark make-up. An avowed Satanist, she proudly described herself as anti-establishment and "goth." During counseling, we often talked about her new-age image, and I asked her why she had dropped out of school.

Cindy said school was just a place that society used to control youth. All adults wanted to do was teach kids to be like them. That way, according to Cindy, society could continue to use everyone. As she explained it, "The businessmen and politicians and religious leaders have gotten together to make us learn what they want. I quit school so I could learn what I want and do what I want. I won't let them train me. I learn by myself, and learn the things that are important to me. I'm an independent woman and I have my own ideas."

Although Cindy claimed to be educating herself according to her own philosophy, her actions spoke louder than her words. Under law, we could not force her to attend class. So, during school, she stayed in her room, watched TV, listened to music, and napped. Outside her room, she visited with staff.

In short, she did everything but work or learn. For Cindy, her professed antipathy to the school establishment was just a convenient way to avoid schoolwork.

꠲

Serious, hard-working, and ambitious, Lisa always did well in school. She excelled in drama, band, and chorus, and her grades were always top-notch. Ginny, Lisa's younger sister, was not interested in studying at all. Blonde, blue-eyed, attractive, and vivacious, she was popular at school, especially with the boys. The girls' parents constantly compared Lisa and Ginny. "Lisa's the smart one and Ginny's the pretty one," they would write in the family newsletters enclosed with Christmas cards.

When Ginny entered high school, competition between the sisters became intense, and their parents didn't help matters with their constant comparisons. While they continually asked Ginny why she couldn't get good grades "like her sister," they wondered aloud when Lisa would "find a nice boyfriend." Ginny was increasingly apathetic towards grades and often claimed that she didn't care if she passed or not.

As Ginny's grades continued to deteriorate, nothing her parents said seemed to encourage her to become interested in school. In fact, in conversations about school, Ginny became passive-aggressive and sarcastic. When grades would come up in a discussion, she would say things like, "Oh, I thought Lisa was the good student. Why don't you ask her about grades?" Or, "I'm just a dumb blonde—what do you expect?"

There is a lot going on underneath Ginny's apparent apathy. Her ambivalence towards school masks a passive aggression based on anger and rebelliousness. She fears failing in the competition between her sister and herself, and avoids competing in academics, where Lisa seems superior. The parents think they are encouraging a healthy sense of competition, but their sibling comparisons are destructive and further provoke Ginny's apathy and underlying passive aggression.

What part of Ginny's apathy is based on the belief that she really can't compete with Lisa academically? What part is projected anger against her parents and their constant comparisons? What part is an excuse for simple laziness? Who knows? Ginny's attitude is a big snarl of mixed motives, unfair biases, peer pressures, and sheer laziness. A tremendous variety of factors can interfere with a healthy attitude towards academics, and these factors can cause a great deal of confusion and frustration among concerned parents.

We have seen how young people can become apathetic towards school because of influence and pressure from peers. We have noted several negative attitudes that can increase apathy and lower grades. But there is one more important factor to consider—the value our youngsters place on education and, especially, graduation from high school.

The devaluation of secondary education. I started attending public high school in 1967. The goal of teenagers in my neighborhood was to finish high school, then to get the good job a high school diploma promised. Still, many people in my neighborhood never finished high school, so graduation was considered quite an accomplishment. In my circle, I was the only one to go on to college. While I spent four years as an undergraduate, my neighborhood pals went to work, got married, and started families. That was their definition of success.

Times have changed. A high school diploma is no longer a means to a solid job. High school graduates may find themselves working in a fast-food restaurant, supervised by a drop-out who started work a few years before them. To get ahead in our modern economy, a college diploma is the minimum requirement, and many good jobs require a degree beyond college. Let's face it—a high school diploma just isn't worth what it once was.

For a teenager entering high school, eight or ten additional years of schooling is a daunting prospect. He or she is already tired of school and sees little economic worth to be gained by continuing his or her education. Four more years for a diploma that does not promise a future seems a poor investment, especially when a job paying real money is available right now. A job is a way to gain status and independence. Many kids have friends who have already dropped out and entered the workforce. Some teens know peers who simply goof off all day and are supported by their parents. Both options seem better than several more years of drudgery and boredom for a diploma that buys nothing.

As you've seen, the roots of apathy run deep. Some youngsters may fear school and avoid going. Others may not see that education helps them reach their goals. Apathy may communicate underlying anger or rebellion. Some kids are just plain lazy. And parents may unintentionally facilitate apathy by defending and rescuing their children. When a youngster's peers also find school worthless and unappealing, it is not hard to see why he or she becomes indifferent towards schooling.

We cannot craft our children's social environment the way we would like, so it may be difficult to destroy the roots of apathy. But we can build character in our children, and doing so will definitely help end the bad grades mess.

Building Character at Home

People who possess character live by principles of behavior that guide their actions. These principles come from attitudes, beliefs, and values that commit the individual to courses of proper conduct. Character is synonymous with integrity and decency. People with character are self-reliant, and are not easily swayed from the right course of action, regardless of what others think.

Character is not instinctive. It is a learned behavior. So, it is important to begin to teach character to our children at an early age. Young people need to learn that principles about right and wrong should guide our lives. They need to learn about the importance of maintaining values in the face of peer pressure. Kids need to learn these lessons over and over again. It is never too early or too late to begin teaching kids about character and integrity.

While working at a local juvenile hall, I listened to a presentation given by a teenage group from Narcotics Anonymous. Five adolescents told the inmates how they came to accept their addiction. They discussed why they decided to change, and how that decision renewed their lives. Three members of the group had been incarcerated at the same facility where they were now speaking. They were proud to come back and admit that they had made bad decisions in their lives. They described a program of change and a course of action.

The recovering addicts were remarkably candid and humble. They all stated that their original mistake was yielding to group pressure, and doing things they knew were wrong to save face with peers. They urged the audience to do what is right, regardless of the social consequences. They said they had developed a new sense of dignity. They said they never wanted to go back to their old ways.

Later, I asked one of these youngsters what had brought about the changes in his character. "While I was in J.V. [juvenile hall]," Josue explained, "I just decided that whatever I was doing, I was doing something wrong. Everybody else was out having a good time and I was locked up. J.V. sucked. My life sucked. I didn't want to ever come back to jail again. I knew I needed to change. I had to grow up. I had to find new friends who'd keep me out of trouble. I had to learn to do the right thing."

Josue's example is instructive for two reasons. First, he was able to see the value of integrity and self-worth. He admitted his wrongs and tried to develop new behaviors. Second, he saw the negative part that his peers had played. He purposely found new friends and formed healthy peer relationships. He overcame peer pressures and did what he felt was right. He was no longer afraid to state his beliefs or to live by them. He found the courage of his convictions—impressive accomplishments for a sixteen-year-old.

It was unfortunate that Josue had to go all the way to juvenile hall before he was willing to change. Had he developed a better sense of character and integrity earlier, he might have avoided a painful, senseless incarceration and a police record.

But we can learn from his mistake and plant the seeds of character in our children. We can begin to build character within our youngsters by openly discussing right and wrong, the impact of peer pressure, and our own family beliefs. We can give them a solid system of values.

Easier said than done? Yes. But we are parents, and it is our job to try. Avoiding such discussions because we assume they will be fruitless is irresponsible. We cannot shirk our parenting duties because we feel uncomfortable or embarrassed.

Instead, we need to make every attempt to build character in our children. We need to start early and never give up on this important task. Whether our children want to listen and learn is not the issue—we need to do our part. We are parents, not entertainers. Raising children who have values and are willing to defend them may be our most important parenting job.

CHAPTER FOUR

Who's in Charge?

*He who takes a stand is often wrong, but he
who fails to take a stand is always wrong.*
—Anonymous

"**W**ho's in charge in your home?" That's a question I often ask parents who come in for help or coaching. Almost always, a parent's immediate reply is, "I am, of course." But, in my experience, many parents are not in charge at all. They have yielded authority and decision-making to a child who holds them as emotional and behavioral hostages. The child intimidates them by withdrawing and acting sullen and surly. The parents struggle to keep the peace, smooth over emerging conflicts, and appease the real boss of the family—the child.

Kristin came home every day after school, immediately walked down the hall to her room, and slammed the door. She remained there until dinner time, when her mother would politely tap on the door and let Kristin know her meal was waiting. Sometimes, Kristin would come out and eat silently, her head bowed over the plate, ignoring everyone. Other times, there was no answer at all from Kristin's room. She would simply stay alone all evening, watching TV, talking on the phone, or listening to music.

On weekends, Kristin would only come out of her room to

41

leave the house with her friends. She would sullenly mention where she was going and stomp out. Later, she would come back, look through the cupboards for a snack, and take it back to her room. Whenever her mother tried to strike up a conversation, Kristin would roll her eyes and walk away. During rare family outings, she would wear headphones and shut out the world. No one at home dared to bother Kristin, and she ignored everyone.

Kristin's parents occasionally tried to improve their relationship with her. Kristin's reply would usually be, "Why don't you leave me alone? I'm not bothering you." Kristin kept curfew and her grades were average. She was never in any real trouble at school, although her teachers complained that she was withdrawn and apathetic. So, her parents didn't feel they had anything tangible to complain about. But Kristin ruled the roost. She acted like she endured her parents' attention. She barely concealed her impatience. She rudely avoided her family and ignored them with impunity.

Who's in charge of this family's home? Not the parents! They walk on pins and needles, fearful of provoking a conflict or somehow intruding on Kristin's imagined "rights" to absolute privacy and complete isolation. At home, Kristin does exactly as she pleases, and her parents conform to her wants and desires. Kristin dictates the rules for interaction and establishes the dynamics of home life for everyone.

How did Kristin's dictatorship come about? When I discussed her behavior with her parents, they said they tried to avoid arguments, did not want to intrude on Kristin's privacy, and, above all, did not want to make her angry. Her mother explained what happened when she crossed Kristin's path:

"Once, when we had guests over, I told Kristin that it was rude for her to stay in her room. I told her she needed to quit moping and come out and spend time with everybody. She was furious. She came out, stomped around in front of the guests, and then sat down, crossed her arms, and just glared at everybody. People would talk to her. She would just stare at them and then turn away. At the dinner table, she ignored everybody and looked out the window. Finally, she asked really loud to be excused and I said, 'Yes, of course.' I just wanted her out of the room. I was completely embarrassed, as were our friends. After that, she didn't talk to us for over a month. She just came home, marched down the hall to her room, and slammed the door. Whenever we said something to her, she hissed, 'Leave me alone. I don't want to talk to you!'

"We just leave her alone. Whenever we try to involve her, or ask her to do anything, she acts like a martyr, rolls her eyes, and stomps around. She never says anything, but gives us this 'I hate you' look. She eats when she wants to and stays in her room. I don't know what she does in there. Whenever I knock on the door, she opens it a crack and peeks out, like I can't come in. I told her once that I felt she was ignoring us. She said, 'So?' and slammed the door."

I have counseled plenty of caring, concerned parents who have somehow been made to feel like they are a bother and an imposition in their own homes. Their children act like living at home is a constant irritant and embarrassment. They think their parents should fulfill their every wish, and at the same time leave them completely alone. These youngsters passively show their anger and displeasure by refusing to talk, avoiding conversations, and isolating themselves.

Yet, they complain constantly. They stake out certain areas of the home, like their bedroom, and act like they hold exclusive rights to them. They claim household goods and treat them like private property. They appear outwardly apathetic, but make it obvious that underlying the feigned indifference is a great deal of latent anger and covert aggression.

Kind, concerned, caring, and sensitive parents are the worst victims of this kind of nonsense because they are the most eager to establish close family bonds with their children. Their children recognize these nurturing instincts and exploit them. They use a passive-aggressive strategy of avoiding and ignoring the family. First, they groan and complain at their every request. Then, in dramatic fashion, they act irritated and frustrated by their parents' apparent foolishness. Passive-aggressive children place the blame for everything squarely on their parents. They themselves are responsible for nothing.

Passive aggression is a very effective tactic. Youngsters who are passive-aggressive communicate several insidious messages to their parents:

❧

"When I act miserable, it's because you're awful parents who make my home life terrible. I'm a cool teen who barely tolerates your idiocy."

"I'm always right and you're always wrong. That's because I'm smart and with-it, and you're old-fashioned, funky, and dumb. I know more than you do."

"All problems between us are your fault. Anytime I'm irritated, it's because you caused it. You need to learn to leave me alone."

"Things have gotten so bad at home that I can barely tolerate living here with you. I'm on the verge of an explosion. Watch out!"

Of course, most children never come right out and say such things—they would sound foolish and immature if they did. That is exactly what makes the passive-aggressive behavior so effective and manipulative. The rudeness and insolence are covert and understated (passive), but the message is crystal clear (aggressive). Passive-aggressive behavior allows children to be unfair and unreasonable without putting themselves in a position where you can call them on it. And, if you did, they would simply huff, ignore you, and withdraw into their rooms.

When faced with indifference and downright hostility from their offspring, many parents panic. They blame themselves. They fear losing their children's affection. They are manipulated into becoming fawning and subservient peacekeepers—exactly what their children intend. Caring, competent parents who succumb to this manipulation surrender control of what happens at home. The entire home scene is scripted and directed by a sullen, withdrawn adolescent.

Parents capitulate because they are afraid of certain things:

- They are afraid of conflict. If I say something, will I cause weeks of sullenness and drama? What if this leads to another explosion?

- They are afraid of noncompliance. What will I do if he simply refuses to follow the rules? If I tell him to do something, and he says "No," what will I do next? What will I do if he runs away?

- They are afraid their child will withdraw affection. Will my daughter hate me? Will she ignore me or leave? Will my son become so angry that I ruin the relationship forever?

- They are afraid to assert themselves. Is it OK to make demands on my child? Am I being old-fashioned, stubborn, unfair, or unreasonable if I do? Am I ruining his or her chance to be special and unique? Is my child right? Are we really that horrible to live with?

Divorced parents face an additional fear. Ex-spouses often compete with one another for the affection of the children. The custodial parent may selfishly or vindictively try to control a child's access to the other parent. The non-custodial parent may try to subvert the rules and regulations of the home, or the authority of the custodial parent. Both parents may try to buy affection or offer bribes for the child's allegiance.

When parents use children as weapons in their own disputes, the children often exploit the competition for their own gain. Many children have gained unfair advantages or manipulated both parents by playing them one against the other, or by threatening to take or change sides. Both parents fear that they will somehow lose access to their children, or that their children will become allied with their ex-partner against them.

Parents' fears paralyze them from taking action, so they give in and tolerate rude and sullen behavior from their kids. As the parents begin to capitulate, passive-aggressive youngsters sense the void in authority, and commence making rules for everybody.

"Nobody can go in my room."
"I get to watch my TV show when it comes on."
"Leave my stuff alone."
"What I do is none of your business."

If their rules are broken, such children will not hesitate to carry out the latent threat behind passive-aggression—causing a ruckus at home.

Parents who rock the boat may find themselves facing temper tantrums, false accusations, weeks of the "silent treatment," or even overt reprisals. Isn't it curious that many parents have never learned to enforce *their* rules, but their children know exactly how to make and enforce their own rules?

The most startling aspect of the passive-aggressive relationship is that the child may actually come to believe that he or she has the right to dictate terms in the household. Parents who do not adhere to child-established rules are seen as unreasonable and unfair.

Equally amazing is the number of parents who accept the idea that their children can establish home rules that everyone must follow. I know one teenage girl who actually called the police when she came home and discovered her mother in her bedroom. She saw her mother as an intruder in her mother's own home. She was so convinced of the sanctity of her "private" room that she wrongly expected the police to arrest her mother for entering it without authority.

◇

The Dysfunctional Family

The word "dysfunctional" means that something is not operating well. When applied to families, dysfunctionality means that the family is not working right—something is broken and needs to be fixed. Dysfunctional families harbor destructive relationships. Family members become emotionally sick. They compete instead of cooperate. Anger, fear, and resentment replace love, caring, and nurturing as dominant emotions.

Nurturing families and dysfunctional families have identifiable characteristics:

NURTURING	DYSFUNCTIONAL
PEOPLE TALK OPENLY ABOUT THEIR FEELINGS	PEOPLE DON'T DISCUSS HOW THEY FEEL
PEOPLE CAN TALK ABOUT ANYTHING	MANY SUBJECTS ARE AVOIDED
DISCIPLINE INVOLVES CRITICISM AND APPROPRIATE CONSEQUENCES	DISCIPLINE INVOLVES SHAMING AND VENGEFUL PUNISHMENTS
CONFLICTS ARE RESOLVED	CONFLICTS ARE AVOIDED
THE HOME ATMOSPHERE IS RELAXED	THE HOME ATMOSPHERE IS STRAINED AND TENSE
ENERGETIC: THINGS GET DONE	LISTLESS: THINGS ARE PUT OFF OR IGNORED
INDIVIDUAL DIFFERENCES ARE ACCEPTED	EVERYONE MUST CONFORM TO THE IDEAS AND RULES OF THE STRONGEST PERSON
PEOPLE COOPERATE AND SHARE	PEOPLE CONTROL AND SUBVERT
PEOPLE TALK FREQUENTLY	PEOPLE SELDOM COMMUNICATE
PARENT-CHILD COALITIONS	PARENT VS. CHILD COMPETITION
PEOPLE ACCEPT RESPONSIBILITY	PEOPLE BLAME OTHERS
PEOPLE WANT TO BE TOGETHER	PEOPLE AVOID EACH OTHER

Dysfunctional families spawn passive-aggressive personalities. Passive-aggression allows a family member to dominate the dynamics of the home and gain the upper hand because the other family members are unwilling to express their feelings, and try to avoid conflicts. If a child emerges as the dominant personality, as is often the case, the entire family becomes passive and intimidated. Parents are tense and confused by their apparent surrender to such a young adversary.

But, they surrender anyway because they are afraid of causing a battle by exercising their rights and meeting their responsibilities. It is easier to blame someone else, ignore the problem, or feign helplessness. So, the manipulation and intimidation continue unabated.

⬥

For many years, it was apparent to everyone that Jackie's marriage was in trouble. She and her husband fought constantly. They seldom spoke except to argue and blame. Their four children, aware of the parents' marital problems, stayed away from home as much as possible. Their grades were horrible, but Jackie was too busy trying to patch up her own problems to help them with theirs. After Jackie filed for divorce, however, she expected things to change.

I met Jackie soon after her divorce. She had found a job and received custody of the four children—a nine-year-old boy and three teenage girls. She immediately established rules and a curfew, insisted that the kids help out around the house, and demanded that they take school seriously. At first, things ran smoothly, but then the girls began to chafe under Jackie's strict guidelines. The daughters became confrontational, then withdrawn and sullen. They threatened to go live with their father, but Jackie refused to allow it.

As she increased the number of rules, and began to administer consequences, the daughters became fed up and took action. The oldest girl, who was the ringleader, called Child Protective Services, and Jackie was summoned before the Family Court to respond to criminal allegations of abuse and neglect brought by her daughters.

To the judge, Jackie honestly and openly explained her new rules and strict policies. She recounted her daughters' demands and passive-aggressive behavior. Although the children claimed horrible abuse, a few minutes of interrogation by the judge revealed their lack of credibility. Jackie was acquitted, but the children were sent to live with their father. Each side claimed victory—Jackie had refused to budge and was exonerated. The girls "got her in trouble" and were allowed to live with their father.

Months later, I saw Jackie again. She mentioned that her three daughters were staying with her "for the summer." For the oldest girl, Jackie had found a job with her company. The other two were enjoying a leisurely vacation at Jackie's apartment. Jackie explained that the girls had avoided her for a few months, then began to come over for weekend shopping and visits. Jackie began to give them gifts and an allowance, and the occasional visits turned into a long-term stay in Jackie's home.

When I spoke to Jackie, her daughters had not been home with their father in months, and had no plans to leave her apartment. Although she was still paying child support, and their father still retained custody, the girls had moved their clothes and possessions back into Jackie's home.

After months of passive-aggressive behavior, criminal charges, and perjury, not to mention manipulation, exploitation, and abandonment, Jackie's daughters were taking advantage of her once again. Why did she

STEPHEN SCHMITZ, PH.D.

allow it? When I asked Jackie about this, she acknowledged that she was being manipulated. When I encouraged her to send the children back to their father, she admitted that she was actually very afraid of the girls. She thought they might start an argument or cause her additional problems. She didn't want to raise a ruckus. As Jackie put it,

> *"We are getting along better now, and the girls want to come over more. I know that they really did some wrong things, but that's OK. I just want things to get back to normal. I want to have a normal relationship with my kids. As long as I don't have problems with them, we get along fine. They can stay at my house as long as they like. Maybe I should be mad and not trust them. I don't know. I just don't want to have problems with them anymore."*

Jackie will not have problems with her daughters anymore—unless she crosses them. She seems to have sold out, ignoring their misbehavior and noncompliance, but benefiting, as she puts it, because she "won't have any problems with them." Then, everybody will "get along fine"—if you overlook the fact that Jackie's kids committed perjury in an attempt to have her thrown in jail, and are doing whatever they want in her home. But, if Jackie decides to put her foot down and enforce some rules or make demands on the girls, it is likely that her children will respond with tantrums, attacks, and reprisals. After all, these tactics worked for them the first time.

In dysfunctional families, members often emulate the more undesirable behaviors of each other. Destructive attitudes and immature actions seem practically infectious. Nowhere is this more apparent than with siblings. Did you notice how Jackie's oldest daughter incited the others to rise up against their mother? As is often the case, the younger children saw the oldest sibling acting out, and decided it was OK to follow suit. The oldest child, bolstered by the support of the others, dared to be even more subversive and disobedient. It became easier for Jackie's oldest daughter to call CPS because she felt she had her younger sisters behind her. They, in turn, were emboldened by her actions.

In families with several children, older siblings who set a bad example are a real problem. Younger siblings can be drawn into undesirable behavior by a misplaced desire to emulate older brothers and sisters. The younger siblings watch the older ones getting away with misbehavior. They see how their parents respond. They learn when and how to test limits.

⬫

Jeffrey and Michael were brothers, born only two years apart. From early childhood, Jeffrey adored his older brother, and was quick to follow his example. The two first got into trouble together when Michael was only nine-years-old. He goaded Jeffrey into sneaking with him into a neighbor's small travel trailer and trashing the interior. They got caught, and Jeffrey immediately blamed Michael for "making him do it." His parents punished Michael severely.

The incident was the first of many similar misbehaviors by the brothers. Vandalism, shoplifting, drunkenness, school fights—the boys always seemed to get caught together, and Michael was always blamed for his brother's misbehavior. After all, he was the older brother and he was "the responsible one." Jeffrey was always just a goofy tag-along, involved in everything but responsible for nothing. The boys' parents always blamed the one son and pardoned the other. They never took control of the situation or tried to intervene—it was easier just to put Michael in charge, and blame and punish him when things went wrong.

When Michael was seventeen, he ran away from home, and was not heard from for several years. Jeffrey, left to his own devices, soon went completely out of control. He quit school, and was explosive and violent with his parents. He was arrested for drug charges, then burglary, and then assault, all in just a few months. He jumped bail and became a fugitive. He was finally caught and locked up.

Jeffrey lost self-control and was arrested because, in childhood, he never had to face the consequences of his behavior. While Michael was learning that punishments quickly follow misconduct, Jeffrey was learning that he could perform misdeeds with impunity. He watched his older brother—his idol—disobey laws, break rules, cheat others, and use drugs. But he never experienced what Michael experienced—the consequences of his misbehavior.

So, whose fault are Jeffrey's wrong turns? Jeffrey certainly deserves a portion of the blame—after all, he was the miscreant. Michael was responsible because he led his impressionable brother along the path of misconduct.

But the parents deserve a great portion of the blame. They abdicated their responsibility. They made Michael responsible for his brother's behavior instead of shouldering the responsibility themselves. They refused to take charge and fix the problem, even after the gravity of the boys' misconduct became obvious.

Accepting the Responsibilities of Parenthood

Underlying each of the examples in this chapter is the same common problem. Parents who should have taken charge in their homes instead surrendered in the face of adversity. They knew something was grievously wrong, but were too intimidated or too frightened to insist that their children comply with their expectations. The parents feared confrontation, abandonment, or legal action. Whatever the fear, they would not or could not confront their own children.

Yet, if our job as parents is to teach our children integrity and character, aren't we obliged to confront them about their misbehavior? Aren't we being irresponsible when we avoid these confrontations because of discomfort and fear? Let's face it, if we are avoiding confrontations with our children, we really aren't doing a very good job of parenting.

Good parents have conflicts with their kids—it's part of the job. The trick is not to avoid conflicts, but to *manage* them positively. Nurturing, healthy families express attitudes and beliefs honestly and openly. They thrash out disagreements, and then clear the air. They forge compromises and accept responsibilities. They use conflicts to resolve differences and improve relationships. Conflict, then, becomes a positive force and a constructive tool, not a negative threat used to shut down communication and to bully family members.

What is the moral of our story? As a parent, you must accept the inevitability of conflict with your children. You must confront youngsters about their behavior and accept your job in molding it. You must never allow your children to do the wrong thing, or ignore their unacceptable behavior, because you want to avoid a confrontation. Instead, you must face the problem. Conflicts are not fun, but they *are* necessary.

Passive Aggression and the Apathetic Underachiever

As you read the section on passive-aggressive behavior, I hope you noticed several behaviors that might apply to your apathetic under-achiever. You may have seen some familiar behavior in the characteristics of dysfunctional families, too. And, as you pondered the list of things parents fear in passive-aggressive relationships, you might have noticed some concerns that keep you from confronting your child about bad grades. Not all apathetic underachievers have passive-aggressive personalities, but passive-aggression and indifference towards academics frequently occur together.

Overt apathy about grades is more than a simple lack of interest. Kids who cop an apathetic attitude about their studies are often acting in a passive-aggressive manner. They avoid dealing with their parents' expectations and concerns. They challenge their parents' right to intervene. They count on the fact that their parents will see the problem, but be too intimidated to do anything about it. They assume that their parents will ignore the grades mess in order to maintain the fragile peace at home. And they often create a myth of superiority, and then actually come to believe that it is true. Their passive-aggression increases as they convince themselves that their actions are right and justified.

The solution, of course, is to stop being intimidated. Accept your parenting responsibilities and take back your authority in your home. Decide to do something about the grades mess, and decide to do something about the manipulation, the intimidation, and the snotty attitude, too.

Jackie never recaptured control over her children because she could never summon the courage to step forward and take charge. Her guilt, fear, and self-doubt overwhelmed her sense of responsibility.

Learn from her mistake. If a passive-aggressive child has taken over your home and stolen your peace of mind, take them back. Don't avoid the confrontation. Manage the conflict calmly and responsibly. Use it to cause changes and fix problems.

You are the parent—take charge of your home.

CHAPTER FIVE

Bad Grades and Bad Attitudes

In America, the young are always ready to give to
[their elders] the full benefits of their inexperience.
—Oscar Wilde

Real change is never easy. We keep to our routines because they are comfortable and help simplify our lives. They provide a sense of constancy and security, and allow us to concentrate our time and energy on what we view as most important. So, changing routines is especially uncomfortable and difficult. The worn saying "old habits die hard" is accurate. Yet, changing routines is exactly what this book asks you to do.

If we are dissatisfied with our lives, thinking about changing to more productive patterns of behavior is easy. But, like my friend Barbara, whom I mentioned in Chapter 1, thinking and reading about self-help is easier than actually putting into practice ideas for positive change. We fall into the trap of procrastination, vowing daily to change uncomfortable situations and negative behaviors tomorrow, or we begin a program of change, work on it for a few days, and then throw in the towel when things do not immediately improve.

✦

Sylvia was an adolescent client of mine who was self-conscious about her weight. She complained about feeling sluggish and wanted to improve her health and appearance by getting into better physical shape. She admitted to me that she had often considered dieting and exercise, but had never really gotten around to making a decision to begin. We decided that if she was truly fed up with her appearance, the best solution was an immediate, rigorous course of action. She began to watch her eating habits, read a book on diet and nutrition, put an exercycle in her living room, and exercise daily. After four months, she had lost six pounds, and suddenly announced her decision to quit the revitalization program. Sylvia was discouraged because she had not already reached her weight loss goals.

She had started out well. She quit procrastinating and began a course of action. She made steady progress towards reasonable goals, yet she gave up because she was impatient with the rate of change. She envisioned herself as slender and vital, but became discouraged when her vision did not become a reality after only four months. Sylvia's *goals* were not unreasonable, but her *timeline* was. She failed to reach her goals because she expected quick perfection instead of steady progress, and she was unwilling to patiently wait for the miracle of her new self to emerge.

Sylvia's story contains two valuable lessons. She was initially successful because she made a decision and acted on it. It is important that you, too, decide on a course of action and begin immediately. However, Sylvia was eventually unsuccessful in maintaining her weight loss program because she gave up too soon. Don't give up before the miracle happens. Once you commit yourself to action, stay the course until you reap the rewards. Change takes time—be patient.

In making your decision, it might be helpful to review some of the progress you have made so far in the book. You have already thought about whether you are fed up with your child's school performance and the negative impact it is having on your life. You have realized that arguments, nagging, blaming, and excuses for poor performance have solved nothing. You have seen the negative role that some peers and passive-aggressive behavior can play in school apathy. You have learned that relying on the school to intervene is unrealistic and that you will have to take charge yourself if things are going to get better. You have read how others, wanting to change, made plans, and imagined how their new, improved lives might be, but never got around to making a concrete decision to begin. You have learned that many others who aspire to real change in their lives fall by the wayside because they do not have the tenacity and patience to stay the course.

Tackling the Attitude Problem

I believe that virtually all K-12 students, except those with a severe learning or physical disability, are capable of doing well in school. School is simply not that hard. The curriculum in most American public schools is far from challenging. If your son or daughter is not faring well academically, the issue is probably more an attitude problem than an intellectual deficit. Your child's perceptions about school and his or her place in it are a greater factor in achievement than skill level, intellect, or preparation. Your child's grades won't change until the attitudes do.

Several sorts of destructive attitudes appear commonplace among underachievers:

Perceptions of a lack of efficacy. Efficacy refers to our ability to do things well and accomplish our tasks successfully. People with high efficacy are productive individuals. When students think they lack academic efficacy, they also believe they cannot succeed—cannot accomplish the goals set for them in the classroom. Each failure is seen as further proof of incompetence. Each bad grade reaffirms what the student has believed all along—that she or he is no good at school. Discouragement leads to apathy, a lack of motivation, and a downward spiral that becomes a self-fulfilling prophecy.

We all have examples from our lives when we have avoided doing something, or done it half-heartedly, because we thought we were not good at it. Here is an example from my own life:

When I first entered college at Colorado State University, I discovered that three semesters of organized physical education coursework were required. Volleyball, a coeducational course, met the requirement, and friends suggested that the class was full of attractive freshmen women, and so I decided to enroll. After a few weeks, it became obvious to me that I was simply no good at the sport. Although I enjoy athletics, I just couldn't get the hang of the game. I felt foolish in class. I resented the exams and skills tests. Learning about the diameter of the ball, the size of the court, and the history of the sport seemed a silly waste of time to me. I suspected one of the other players of cheating. I quickly decided that the instructor was not very good. I began to grumble to myself even as I headed to class. Volleyball class became a chore.

As I look back on my college volleyball experience, however, several things seem clear. My perception of inadequacy became a self-fulfilling prophecy. The volleyball class was not particularly difficult. In fact, it was far easier than most of my other coursework. Realistically, I played about as well as most of the beginners did. There was actually not much information to learn, and classes mostly consisted of playing matches in mixed teams with attractive coeds.

I should have enjoyed myself, yet I became disenchanted with volleyball class because of my misplaced perception that I was not good at the game. Because I didn't immediately become an expert player, I was self-conscious and uncomfortable in class. I soon began to minimize the value of the course. I blamed the instructor. I became apathetic. My attitude about my efficacy as a volleyball player became destructive to my own progress.

Passive victimization. Teri, a dear friend's daughter, came to visit us one Christmas. Home from her first year at the University of Texas, she told all of us about the new and exotic foods she had tried in Austin, the exciting nightlife there, and all the interesting new friends she had gained at school, including a charming and attentive boyfriend. An unassuming girl from a small town, she had become socially alive at college and found a comfortable niche in the university community.

Yet, Teri, who had been an outstanding student and a scholarship winner in high school, had managed only mediocre marks after two university semesters. We suspected she might have gone overboard on the college social scene. She, on the other hand, saw herself as a victim of the academic environment. As Teri explained it,

❂

"I have to take a lot of classes that I don't really like and that have nothing to do with my major. They take up a lot of my time. The general education classes are too big and the professors are boring. So, the classes are monotonous and it's hard to pay attention and study. The teachers aren't clear at all and it's hard to keep track of exactly what's going on in class. They just stand there and lecture and go off into their own little thing. I don't know what I expected, but some of the professors are really not teaching me very well."

If you read Teri's comments attentively, you probably recognized the excuses and blaming that often accompany underachievement. What really comes through in Teri's story, however, is her belief that she is somehow a victim of the educational establishment. It's all about them, and has nothing to do with her. She sees her learning role as that of a passive observer who should be challenged and entertained by her professors. According to Teri, if she is not learning, it is because the school is not doing its job—and whose fault is that? She complains, "They are not teaching me well," instead of admitting, "I am not learning well." The time spent on her new community involvement, romantic interests, and social life do not seem to enter into her thinking at all.

Work should have an immediate payoff. Another destructive attitude common among underachievers is that they should have to do something only if an immediate reward is forthcoming. Unfortunately, the school and home may perpetuate this attitude by rewarding behavior that should be expected.

❁

I often work in a classroom at a local children's home. In a wonderful program called Silent Sustained Reading (SSR), 30 minutes daily are set aside for the children to quietly read whatever they choose. The regular classroom teacher awards points to those students who manage to complete their daily SSR, and the kids eagerly comply because the points can be exchanged for prizes, such as stuffed animals and toys. Since I do not reward the students with such points, it is quite difficult to get them to read for me, even though some students admit they love to read. The problem is that they have learned to read only for a reward, and when the payoff is not forthcoming, the reading stops.

For most mature adults, the rewards of hard work at school are apparent in future gains. Academic success translates into better life chances, higher earnings potential, and a more promising career. The principle that we should work hard now in order to reap rewards later is called deferred gratification, and youngsters are notoriously bad at postponing rewards, because they live entirely in the present. The notion of future rewards in adulthood is a highly abstract idea, and children, until late adolescence, think poorly in the abstract. To them, earning a livelihood as an adult is a challenge millions of years in the future, but school chores exist as a dreary fact of daily current life.

Similarly, as mentioned in Chapter 2, children often fail to see any connection between hard work, deferred gratification, and success in life. In a bizarre twist of logic, many adolescents operate under the sad assumption that if they want something, and others have it, then the world should automatically provide it to them. Many youngsters pursue this sense of entitlement through the gates of adult underemployment or poverty.

My behavioral client, Ashley, a bright and articulate fourteen-year-old, was trying to explain to me why she didn't feel the need to do well in school:

✧

"Well, I want to be a singer, either in a band or by myself, and I don't need to go to school to do that. I know that everybody wants to be a singer, but I'm really good and I think I can do it. It'll be fun and I'll make a lot of money. I know it'll take me awhile to get established and for people to get to know me, but I'll find someone to take care of me until I can make some money and take care of myself. After that, I'll hire somebody else to handle the money and stuff."

Ashley's sense of entitlement, her belief that she should get to be a rock star, that it should happen just because she wants it to, and that someone should take care of her until she succeeds, is surprisingly typical of the teenagers with whom I work. School and hard work are not necessary—things will happen because they are supposed to.

Teri's and Ashley's stories also reveal another attitude that I find common among underachievers. They believe that if they find an activity like work unrewarding or boring, they should not have to do it.

"If it's not fun, I don't have to do it." I met Amy through her mother, a professional colleague. Amy was a bright, buoyant, athletic ninth grader who enjoyed sports and was quite popular around her small Texas town.

✵

After her parents' divorce, Amy moved in with her father, who works long hours during the day. Poorly supervised, she became dissatisfied with the "boredom" of school and simply quit going. Amy's father was gone before she got up in the morning, and no one made sure she went to classes. When the school called, no one was home to answer. After several months of this, the father was served with a truancy warrant. Incredibly, Amy, her father, and the school counselor jointly decided that if Amy did not like school, she would not have to go! They arranged a home-schooling program, where she stayed at home all day, alone and without supervision, supposedly doing the work she found boring while in school.

Amy started her home-schooling course with enthusiasm and diligence. Soon, however, she was making little progress with her coursework. Without supervision, she lost interest in her assignments. Her boyfriend, a nineteen-year-old school drop-out, began to come over during study time. Needless to say, she didn't get much work done. Within four months, the entire course was in a closet and Amy was done with home-schooling.

One interesting aspect of this story is Amy's attitude: because school was not entertaining, she simply wouldn't go. More significant are the supposedly responsible adults who caved in to that sort of decision, based on that kind of thinking. You might have scoffed at my generalization about adolescents who simply expect something to happen because they want it so, but isn't this exactly what happened in Amy's case? And, didn't the adults around her buy into her sense of entitlement, allowing her to do whatever she wanted, just because she wanted to do it? Doesn't it seem that the adults gave in to placate her, avoid a confrontation, and ignore their responsibility for managing her education? Certainly, everyone involved in Amy's case accepted the premise that school was not right for Amy, simply because she did not like it.

Amy's failure with schooling was compounded by her father's failure at parenting. He was as irresponsible as she was because he took the easy way out to avoid a confrontation. Confronting Amy and demanding that she responsibly attend school was her father's job, and he failed at it abysmally. He should have stepped forward with a sense of courage and accepted the authority in their relationship, even if it caused a conflict. Instead, Amy gambled that he would abdicate responsibility, and, as she expected, she would win out. Because of his abdication, she got exactly what she wanted.

The Myth of Intelligence. Many children, and their parents, believe that the students who perform the best in school are the brightest. In its simplest form, the assumption is that the smartest kids get the best grades, and the kids of lower intelligence earn the poorest grades.

Nothing could be farther from the truth! Albert Einstein, for example, was an awful student. Winston Churchill suffered from severe learning disabilities.

Educational researchers have repeatedly demonstrated that high grades are a function of several factors, and that smart kids do not necessarily get better grades. In fact, some studies have suggested that those students who get superior grades in elementary school are the best-behaved students, not those who learn the most. A student with marginal ability and a strong work ethic will certainly fare better in most American schools than a student who is bright but lazy.

I first learned this lesson from my nephew, Matt, a big, good-natured youngster with a quick, goofy smile whom everyone seemed to like.

✦

Matt struggled throughout elementary school. His close-knit family was concerned about his low grades at school, and saddened by his apparent frustration. Finally, an alert school counselor identified Matt as dyslexic. Still, for years, Matt continued to grapple with mediocre grades and constant frustration, and everyone assumed that things would always be this way because of his "below average intelligence" and "learning disability."

Then, in high school, Matt suddenly and inexplicably decided that he wanted to become a teacher. He developed a passion for school, and his grades shot up. Matt became excited about his classes and started looking into colleges. He changed from a lethargic learner into a solid achiever, all because his desire to excel overcame his supposed lack of intelligence, his dyslexia, and his self-perceived inability to compete. Now, Matt has a classroom of his own and works to motivate other slow learners.

Matt turned out to be a great deal more intelligent than anyone imagined. He was successful as soon as he quit buying into the notion that he was incapable of doing well in school. He stopped making excuses and started learning. While everyone else saw reasons why Matt couldn't achieve, he saw reasons why he could. All it took was a change in attitude.

Many underachievers are held back by such false attitudes and beliefs. All these different destructive attitudes, often found in underachievers, have things in common. In every case, the student:

• *makes external excuses*
• *feigns helplessness or incompetence*

- *blames everyone but himself or herself for his or her shortcomings*
- *becomes apathetic and refuses to participate*
- *rationalizes unacceptable beliefs and behaviors*

But while Amy's father bought into her rationalizations and destructive attitudes, *you* don't have to. Like Matt, you can get busy and change things. You can accept the fact that something is seriously wrong, that whatever you are doing right now is not working, and that you need to take charge to fix things.

An important first step towards solving the problem is to get rid of your old, unproductive attitudes about your child's underachievement. Begin your attitudinal housecleaning by focusing on your own needs instead of your child's. Assert your rights and obligations as a parent. Then, accept the responsibility of being the agent of change.

◇

This is Your Problem

It is important to realize why underachievement is your problem. It is not because you are to blame. Nor is it because you are guilty of poor parenting. You have probably spent many a sleepless night pondering why your child is failing to measure up, and what you can do about it. You have bent over backwards to be accommodating. Your child's school performance has affected your life in negative ways, causing you stress and anxiety, leading to arguments at home, and leaving you feeling manipulated, taken advantage of, and used. Your child has ignored you, his teacher has blamed you, and you have often blamed yourself for your child's failings. Although your child's lack of achievement is not your fault, it definitely is your problem, because it is causing you anxiety and making you unhappy.

Look at this selfishly for a moment. Why should you be required to put up with this nonsense? Is tolerating awful grades and negative attitudes part of your job as a parent? If anyone is a victim here, it is *you*. You haven't done anything wrong. In fact, you have probably given the matter your best efforts. Your child's problem is becoming your problem because it is affecting your life in negative ways and interfering with your contentment and peace of mind. That is not fair to you.

It is OK to be selfish. Being a good parent does not mean letting your kid's grades ruin your peace of mind and sense of well-being. You have the responsibility to intervene because it's your life and you are responsible for it. Taking charge of your child's education means taking responsibility for *your* life, happiness, and peace of mind. It means resolving to not let the actions or situations of others interfere with *your* emotional health. Your child's grades are driving *you* crazy, and *you* have the right to your sanity.

A good place to begin a program of change is within. A careful examination of some of *your* attitudes, beliefs, and values is appropriate. Too often, people dissatisfied with certain aspects of their lives are convinced that everything will be better if only they can change the behavior of someone else. We become victims of the delusion that our lives are awful because of someone else's behavior, and that if we only could change the other person, our lives would greatly improve somehow.

We see ourselves as emotional hostages. We fool ourselves into believing we are helpless victims of the behavior, or misbehavior, of others. But we do not have to be victims. Each of us has the right to manage our own life in our own best interests. All we have to change is our attitude.

I now want to add an important new idea to our list of principles:

The most important attitude to change is yours.

CHAPTER SIX

Ten Things Parents Do Wrong

There is nothing sadder than an old hipster.
—Lenny Bruce

A n important avenue of change is creating a home-school alliance. However, this step will bring results only if you combine it with other changes at home. You will have to take action to improve the home environment as a base of academic performance. You will have to look at your relationship with your child, and at how you both view rewards and responsibilities. You will certainly have to revamp some of your deeply held beliefs about child rearing and your role as a parent.

But first, let us take a few moments to examine some of the things you may be doing as a parent that contribute to the problem. You probably won't be doing all of these things, but see if a few of them sound familiar. While reading about these problems, keep in mind that the blaming game is over. There is no reason to feel guilty or defensive about your past efforts with your children. You have undoubtedly done your very best. We only want to examine ways to improve the situation so we can solve the bad-grades problem.

Parents think they should be selfless. Many parents believe that parenting entails some sort of martyrdom that requires them to sacrifice everything for the sake of their kids. These parents "go without" so their

71

children can have the very best of everything. You can pick out these parents by their favorite saying, "I want him to have all the things I never had when I was a kid." Some of these parents may resent their self-imposed sacrifices, but most of them actually feel a sense of pride in their ability to provide what they see as the very best for their child. What they fail to realize is that, unintentionally, they may be teaching their children the wrong lessons by their generosity.

✢

I met Anne when she lived in a small Texas town with her two teenage daughters. A single mother with many friends and family in other areas of the state, she was often forced to travel because of her job. Because of work-related travel undertaken during the winter, she would sometimes feel the need to stay the night at her friends' homes, fearful of driving slick Texas rural roads alone late in the evening.

Although she bought her older daughter a car, Anne would frequently get up at 4:30 a.m. and drive the 60-70 miles back home so she could take her younger daughter to school. Her daughters both lived within two miles of their schools, and the county provided school bus service. Yet, Anne did not want to inconvenience either of her youngsters by making them share a ride or take the bus. She was afraid that if she asked the older daughter to drive the other to school, "She'll throw a fit, and they'll fight all the way there." For Anne, her willingness to make the long drive back home early in the morning was an indication of her dedication as a parent, and a sign she would sacrifice her own well-being for her children.

In this instance, Anne's sacrifice involved, in part, the gift of the car, but also the sacrifice of her time and effort in what she saw as her daughters' behalf. What Anne failed to see is that she was teaching the wrong lessons to her children. They were learning that:

- You don't have to do anything to get a car. The car, as well as the payment of its expenses, are your right without obligation.

- Arguing with your sister is good and productive. Mother will intervene and let you have your way in order to avoid a conflict.

- It is normal and justifiable to expect other people to spend excessive time, money, and energy to serve you. You deserve it.

- If your mother has always done something for you, you are entitled to the service forever.

- If you act helpless, Mom will step in and solve your problems.

- Your convenience and your priorities come before those of anyone else. It is OK to be self-centered.

Anne's daughters never thanked her for driving home so early and so far every morning. They called friends' homes demanding to know where she was and when she was coming back. They claimed that Anne was irresponsible to leave them alone, although they often babysat other parents' children. They complained about her absence, about the "old car" she had left them with, and about having to wait for a ride. They felt entitled to her services because, in the past, she had always driven them to school.

Anne's daughters wanted it both ways—they wanted to be treated like responsible adults, but they also wanted to be cared for like children. I urged Anne to help them grow up by insisting that they assume some of the responsibility for managing their own lives. I also encouraged Anne to recognize the girls' whining and complaining as a form of manipulation, intended to intimidate her into doing things for them that they should, and could, do for themselves. I told her to quit feeling guilty and to put herself first for a change.

The subtlety of Anne's predicament is that, by struggling to be a good parent, she actually hindered the girls' emotional development. They learned all the wrong lessons and became increasingly self-centered. In the short term, Anne showed her dedication and caring. But in the long term, she taught the girls that through intimidation and playing the victim, they could con other people into taking care of them. So, they became more adept at manipulating people than accepting responsibility.

This became apparent to me about three years later when I had the opportunity to talk to her younger daughter again. Now sixteen-years-old, Erin was ready to drop out of school because she wanted to get married. Her boyfriend was moving to another state, and she decided to accompany him. According to Erin, they would get married "later." When I asked Erin about her plans for her future, she explained that she was tired of school and wanted to settle down and be a homemaker. Her comments are enlightening:

> *"I want to get married, and then stay home. I don't want to work. Tommy, my boyfriend, can take care of us and make the money. I can stay at home and do the things that I want. Mom*

thinks I'm too young to get married, but I don't care. There's noth-
ing she can do to stop me. I'm old enough to live by myself and do
whatever I want. We won't have a lot of money to start, but we'll
live with his brother until Tommy can find a job. His family can help
out and his mom says she'll put him through plumbers' school if he
wants. His family will take care of us until we get settled."

Most sixteen-year-old girls think they are too young to accept the responsibilities of marriage, but Erin has no experience with responsibility. She doesn't have a clue about what an adult lifestyle entails. Did you notice how often she refers to what "I want"? She envisions an adulthood where a caregiver always supports her, handles her affairs, and manages her life. She expects a carefree future where a family member or boyfriend handles all the responsibility, and she is free to do whatever she wants. After all, this has been Erin's experience, virtually from childhood. Why should she expect things to change? Marriage, motherhood, and maturity seem easy when you never have to deal with responsibility.

The story of Anne and her daughters also spotlights a second, rather familiar error common among parents:

Parents give in to keep the peace. Have you ever noticed how, with your kids, little disagreements can quickly turn into big brawls? Some children have found that their parents will passively yield to their demands instead of saying "no" and precipitating an argument. Kids who argue about everything do so because they have learned that parents will back off, or simply ignore issues, in order to keep peace in the household. In Anne's case, the arguing between her teenagers had become such an irritant that she was willing to drive 70 miles every morning in order to keep them from quarreling about rides to school.

You may remember Amy, whom we met in Chapter 5 after she refused to go to school. In another episode drawn from her life, her father failed to ask some important questions because he wanted to avoid a conflict, worrying more about the consequences of confronting her than the consequences of not adequately supervising her.

⊰⊱

Amy was notorious for doing what she wanted, and for arguing when she didn't get her way. Her single father seemed to have given up. She reported to me once that she had gone to spend the week with her eighteen-year-old boyfriend while his parents were away. I asked what her father had thought about her spending an entire week in her boyfriend's home. Amy said she had simply told her father, "Dad, I'm going to spend the week with Jason at his house. His parents say it's OK." Dad paused, then shrugged his shoulders, and replied, "Well, I guess if it's OK with them, it's OK with me."

In this instance, the failure of Amy's father to ask some tough questions about the details of her weeklong sleepover bordered on child neglect. To get her way, she cagily exploited his habit of avoiding conflict. Her father covered himself by deferring to the other parents' wishes (who, it turns out, actually knew nothing about these plans), purposefully remaining ignorant of her true intentions. He preferred to ignore his parenting responsibilities instead of provoking a clash of wills. So, Amy won by default.

Like other parents whose stories we have analyzed, Amy's father took the easy way out. He avoided conflict and thereby abdicated his parenting responsibilities. He should have asked tough questions and gotten clear answers. He should have established clear rules about dating. He should have communicated his expectations. He should have done something—anything—except avoid the problem.

Parents treat kids like children. "Shouldn't they?" you ask. "Not always" is my answer. If you believe that children need to learn to accept responsibility so they can competently manage their own lives, it is sometimes wise to let children be responsible for themselves and experience the consequences of their own actions. Certainly, for example, Anne's daughters could have been responsible for getting themselves to school in the mornings. When Anne took that responsibility away from them, they received the wrong message. Parents who do not let their kids grow up and become responsible teach their kids two lessons. The first is *learned helplessness*—the idea that "I cannot do this for myself, and someone has to do it for me." The second lesson is *entitlement*, or, "Someone else is responsible for providing for me and solving my problems."

Remember: rescuing your children teaches them that they can avoid the natural consequences of their actions. Teach kids responsibility by giving them responsibilities. Teach them self-reliance by making them rely on themselves.

Parents try to buy their children's affection. Although they won't want to admit it, many parents buy their children things they do not need, hoping that their generosity will cause their children to appreciate them. Most children are not at all timid about asking their parents to buy them things, and many parents have a hard time saying "no." Sullen, disinterested children can become warm, caring, and attentive when the parent's credit card comes out. For some parents, the only way to convince their kids to spend time with them is to take the kids shopping. And, as we have seen, children are quick to adopt an attitude of entitlement. Yet, children who know how much they like a gift may quickly forget where it came from.

⚓

Alex bought his daughter, Brandy, a cell phone for her twelfth birthday as part of a new multi-phone family plan. Although he carefully explained the charges and time constraints on her phone use, she quickly ran up several hundred dollars on his account. In my office, Alex complained that he felt taken advantage of and used. This was especially irksome to him because he thought he had done something particularly generous by purchasing the phone. I asked Alex point blank what he had expected when he purchased a cell phone for a twelve-year-old. "She really wanted one," he said. "I thought it might prove helpful in case of an emergency, and it would allow her to keep in close contact with me when she was out."

Brandy, interestingly, had already bought into the attitudes of learned helplessness and entitlement. She sat in on the session with me, arms crossed, shoulders hunched, and gave her side of the story: "All my friends have cell phones, and I wanted one, too. I asked for one, and he bought me one. So, I talk a lot on the phone. What does he expect me to do with a phone—not talk on it? I didn't keep track. I didn't know it would cost so much. It's not my fault. If he didn't want me to talk, he shouldn't have bought me the phone."

Brandy's attitude is typical of some teenagers. She is convinced that she is entitled to the phone because everyone else has one. She claims that she is helpless to keep track of her usage and charges. She blames her father for the problem because he bought her the phone. She is unwilling to accept responsibility for her own actions.

Alex, on the other hand, feels like a victim. His daughter blamed him for buying her the phone in the first place, but why did he do it? He wanted to get his daughter an expensive gift, hoping to enhance his image as a "cool" and responsive parent and thus earn her affection. Instead, he was made to appear stingy and indecisive.

I have seen parents buy all sorts of expensive, and inappropriate, gifts for their children—jewelry, sound systems, laptops, and even cars. Often, the parents have a rationalization for the purchase. "He needs it for school," or "She's always wanted it," but these rationalizations are shallow excuses for what often amounts to simple parental insecurity. They buy these things because they are insecure about the relationship they have with their children. They use money to bolster their status with their kids.

Should parents stop buying expensive gifts for their children? No, but they should examine their motives, make sure that they are not being manipulated, and be careful that gift-giving teaches their children the right lessons. Spending money doesn't make you a good parent. The best gift you can give your child is the gift of good parenting.

Parents try to live vicariously through their kids. My mother always says she feels seventy-five on the outside and sixteen on the inside. Deep inside, we all still feel young, but some of us forget that we are neither the friends nor the cohorts of our children.

For many years, I coached junior high school wrestling, and I used to see fathers, years past any semblance of athleticism, trying to relive their youths through their sons' exploits on the mat.

⊃✿⊂

David was the proud parent of our all-district wrestling champion. He was a fanatic at our matches. He sent in notes with his son about the other teams he had scouted for us. He came to wrestling matches wearing his own school-colors uniform. Before each match, he offered his advice and opinions. He rushed to the sidelines when it was his son's turn to wrestle, and several times the referee had to ask him to sit down. David knew the names of all the wrestlers and all the cheerleaders. Everyone always came to his house after matches. Once, when his son was injured, David came to the sidelines and shouted, "Is he seriously hurt? Can he still wrestle?" and, when he saw his son had suffered only a minor injury, complained to me, "What's wrong with you? Why don't you put him back in the match?!"

You have all seen these parents—a loud mother dressed up like her daughter and shopping with her for clothes, a dad who gets overly chummy with his daughters' acquaintances, and parents anxious to show they are still "with it" when their children's friends come over.

⊃✿⊂

Susan was a middle-aged floor supervisor at a Texas discount store. She was extremely proud of her daughters, Andrea and Britney, who were attractive, talented, and popular. Andrea, who had become interested in competitive gymnastics, was a fierce competitor. Britney was more interested in the social aspects of her school life, and was often in the company of her many acquaintances and boyfriends. Susan often bragged about both girls—their successes and their popularity.

Susan stunned me twice during a single conversation about her daughters. Although Andrea was moderately successful in her school gymnastics competitions, she was far from an Olympic hopeful. Yet, Susan announced that she had decided to sell the family home in order to pay for daily professional training for Andrea. "If she was destined to be great," Susan told me, "and I failed to support her, I would never forgive myself." Susan also described how she had been going out in the evenings with Britney, driving up and down the local drag, and taking part in a popular teenage pastime there. Susan was quick to describe all the boys who had slowed down to flirt with "them" and all the fun things she and Britney had done with "the other kids."

I was shocked that Susan found flirting to be an appropriate activity to share with her daughter. I was dumbfounded by her willingness to sacrifice her house for gymnastics lessons. Susan did several things badly. She was selfless and self-sacrificing to an extreme, tried to purchase one daughter's affections, and tried to be "with it" by cruising the strip with her other adolescent youngster.

Being "with-it" is laudable. In fact, I encourage every parent to try to become acquainted with their children's friends. But parents should respect the limits and boundaries of the parent-child relationship. Your kids do not need another friend—they have plenty already. They do not need a patron who shows affection through extravagant buying sprees.

What they need is a firm, caring, responsible adult who can point them in the right direction and serve as a leader in their lives. Parents should be guidance counselors, role models, and teachers, not pals.

Gradebusters

✦

During college, I lived in a large rooming house near campus. It was the 1970s, and in the bohemian atmosphere of the times, there was a live-and-let-live mentality of acceptance and toler-ance. Many of the rooming house residents drank heavily, and most used marijuana on an occasional basis. Back then, no one thought anything of it. I was shocked, however, when one day I entered Pam's room to borrow a book and found her sitting on the bed smoking pot with her parents. "It's alright," she said, "they're cool," responding to my shocked expression. Her parents calmly invited me to participate with them.

I did not participate, and I didn't stick around to be introduced to Pam's parents, either. During the time Pam lived in the rooming house, her parents came to visit on a regular basis, and often got high, visited night clubs, and went partying with their daughter. I never felt comfort-able with them, and neither did anyone else in the house.

It wasn't that they were grown-ups. It was that they were parents, and we expected something different from parents than friends. Pam's family had somehow confused the need to be pals with the responsibil-ities of good parenting.

Most middle-age adults report that they feel younger than they real-ly are. Inside, each of us adults is a youthful spirit with a child-like exu-berance we hope never to lose. Maintaining the vigor of youth is com-mendable, but feeling young does not mean acting immaturely. Celebrate your youthfulness, but act like an adult. Pam's parents never grew up. Furthermore, they committed another error because they failed to act as good role models.

Parents forget to be good role models. The old adage, "Do as I say, not as I do," is nonsense. Our kids constantly learn from us, whether we want them to or not. Unfortunately, it seems, they always notice and internalize the wrong messages. If a mother smokes, can she explain to her daughter why the daughter should not? How can parents who speed expect their kids to drive responsibly?

I suffer from bursitis, which causes my knees to become stiff and inflexible. My girlfriend and I frequently walk along Newport Beach, a popular area for joggers, families with children, and sight-seers. The walk helps loosen my knee joints and restores a degree of flexibility to my sore leg muscles. Along each corner of the Boardwalk and the beach is a clear, posted sign that says, "No Skateboarding on the Boardwalk." Although there are bicycle police along the Boardwalk, skateboarders abound, and the police play a sort of cat-and-mouse game trying to catch the skateboarders.

Along the Boardwalk, we constantly see parents whose children are on skateboards. Parents and kids both seem to ignore the signs. In fact, the parents often serve as lookouts for their skateboarding kids. "Look out!" Dad will caution. "The cops are coming! Get off your board."

We once observed a woman whose son had been stopped by the bicycle patrol. The woman was livid that the police had the temerity to stop and ticket her son for breaking the law. "Don't you police have anything better to do than hassle skateboarders?" she shouted. "Why don't you go catch some burglars or something?"

These parents are scofflaws, plain and simple. The issue is not whether they agree with the law or think it is important. Parents who openly disobey laws in front of their kids raise kids who do the same thing. And, youngsters do not have the intellectual sophistication to decide which laws are important and what their chances are of getting caught. Once they learn that it is OK to break so-called insignificant laws, it is a quick leap to breaking all the laws of their choice.

Parents make a serious mistake when they assume that teaching and learning only occur at arranged times. Kids learn from adults all day long, whether the adults intend it or not. They mimic whatever they see adults doing—good or bad. Research suggests that the children of Republicans tend to be Republicans. Likewise, the children of smokers tend to be smokers, and the sons of wife-beaters grow up to be wife-beaters.

Parents make a grave mistake when they say one thing and do another. They forget that what their children see them do is vastly more important than what their children hear them say.

Parents defend their children's behavior or blame others for it. It is hard to convince a child that his actions are wrong when, like the mother defending the illegal skateboarder, his parent defends him. The child believes that his behavior is acceptable because the parent rationalizes it.

Many years ago, a parent called the junior high school where I was working and complained that I had severely beaten her son, Mike. The day before, I had seen Mike bullying a younger child and confronted him about it. Resentful and vengeful, the son lied to his mother and claimed I had attacked him. Knowing I was a solid teacher, my principal invited the mother to school for a conference

and, in the meantime, began to investigate.

When the mother arrived at the school, the principal was armed with the facts. The principal pointed out that several students and at least two teachers had seen the incident and remembered that I had confronted Mike but never touched him. Many of the students reported that Mike had hurt the smaller child. The other child's mother had already complained to the school.

Mike had a history of bullying at the school and had been caught lying about teachers on other occasions. He was already on behavioral probation. Yet, after all this, the mother continued to claim not only that her son had done nothing, but that he had been brutalized. She vowed to go to the school board to get the principal and I removed. Before that happened, however, Mike was expelled from school after seriously injuring another child with a baseball bat.

This parent's behavior may seem extreme, but is it any different than that of the mother of the skateboarder? In both cases, parents who know that their child was wrong insisted on defending him anyway. Experienced teachers and therapists often see this misplaced loyalty among the parents of troubled kids. Some parents are embarrassed by their children, while others think their child's behavior reflects on them. Some parents are easily lied to by their kids. Parents may believe that defending their offspring, no matter what, is a parental duty.

But, in cases like Mike's, the strategy backfires because the child sees the parent's defense of him as an affirmation of his behavior. So, the child repeats wrong actions over and over again.

Parents wait for change instead of causing it. How many times have you heard parents chalk up their child's rotten behavior to a "stage" they are going through? The "terrible twos" become the "starting school" years, followed by the usual "junior high attitude" and "raging hormones," succeeded by a "boy-crazy" or "girl-crazy" period. Parents continually wait for their child's "stage" to disappear, along with the negative behavior that supposedly accompanies or causes it.

The bad news is that there are no developmental stages that excuse poor behavior or low grades. The only changes that parents can count on are those that they cause. But, the bad news is good news, too, because it means that parents don't have to wait to begin real change. Any time is a good time to start. One important step is to identify the problem. Another solid step is to devise a plan to solve it. But, parents can easily fall down on either count or on both counts.

Parents tend to generalize about their children's problems. Looking back at my clinical notes for this book, I was dumbfounded by the number of parents' sweeping generalizations about their children's misbehavior. For example:

- "Ellie never does her homework."
- "Every day, when Tom gets out of bed, the first thing he does is whine."
- "Sara has never had anything positive to say about school."
- "I don't think Matt will ever be good at school."

Statements that contain words like "never," "always," "ever," and "every day," don't help for two reasons. First, they make the problem seem so big, it is hard to imagine a good solution. Second, they make it unclear what the problem really is. It is important to describe the problems you are having in very specific terms, like:

- "Ellie's teacher called and said she did not turn in her homework yesterday morning."

- "Today, when Tom got out of bed, he complained that he did not feel like going to school."

- "Sara told me after school that her social studies class is difficult and boring."

- "Matt has a D average in math this semester."

The more narrow and descriptive you can make the problem statement, the better. For example:

"I have tried a special education program, a private school, a military academy, and a behavioral class for my son. He has failed each one. I do not know what to try next."

Another important thing to do, after you specifically describe the problem, is to state exactly what you want to happen. Set reasonable goals that your child can accomplish by committing to them. Describe what your son or daughter should actually *do*—something you can see happen.

"I want Elmo to do well in school," if stated as a goal, is of little use for several reasons. It is not a description that focuses on Elmo, because it starts with, "I want . . . " And what does "well" mean? And when should Elmo do this in school? Now? Forever? If we go to Elmo's school, how will we tell if he is doing well or not?

"Elmo will earn a grade of C in mathematics next semester."

Now, that's better! That goal describes exactly what Elmo is supposed to do. It is not subject to interpretation—he either gets the C or he doesn't.

There is also a precise timeline so we know when Elmo is supposed to accomplish his goal.

Finally, the goal is realistic. If Elmo is struggling in math, you just want him to pass. Expecting and insisting on an A+ right away is a recipe for failure.

> *"Tom will stop whining all the time."*

This one has problems, too. What exactly do we mean by "whining?" Does he actually whine *all* the time? Can he stop his behavior? Do you mean that he whines all the time, or that he should stop whining all the time? This goal lacks clarity.

> *"At the breakfast table, Tom will not complain about going to school."*

See? Better. Now we know exactly what the behavior is, and when we want it to stop. We can watch Tom at breakfast and actually see if he is making any progress. These sorts of clearly written goals—those that describe exact behaviors, times, and targets—are called "behavioral objectives." It is important that you begin to think about behavioral objectives.

Parents do not form a plan of action. A military general who starts a battle without a plan is a fool. A builder has a plan before he begins to construct a home. Similarly, you need a plan of action when you begin to reconstruct your child's academic life. A haphazard approach will only lead to a disaster.

⬦

Arnie brought his two teen sons into our behavioral facility after a couple of years of serious trouble with the boys at home and school. His sons had begun to smoke and drink heavily and were arrested together for shoplifting. The police found marijuana in one boy's pocket. Arnie, a fundamentalist Christian, took parenting seriously and was not afraid to mete out discipline. He was devastated, for he saw the sinful ways of his children, and was willing to do anything to help change their behavior.

Arnie and I carefully reviewed what he had tried so far: discussions, threats, grounding, loss of TV and phone privileges, extra housework, family prayer, school counseling—but nothing had seemed to work. Arnie was fed up. He freely admitted that he had run out of ideas. He wanted me to "fix" his kids, and was disappointed when I told him I couldn't do so.

I remember Arnie well because he was a caring, likeable man who seemed genuinely concerned for the welfare of his children. He wanted answers, and was willing to work with his sons to implement changes. I suggested two principles to Arnie. I think they are good principles for all of us to follow:

Decide exactly what you want to have happen with the behavior of your kids.

Implement a concrete, coordinated plan of action.

CHAPTER SEVEN

Rights, Responsibilities, and Good Parenting

Discussion is an exchange of knowledge.
Argument is an exchange of ignorance.
—Robert Quillen

Many parents complain to me that they have lost control of their children, and do not know what to do about it. They fear that, as parents, they no longer have the legal right to discipline their children or control their behavior. They somehow believe that, if they try to discipline their children, the children can refuse to cooperate, and continue to "do whatever they feel like." Some even tell me that, if they try to punish their children, a protective agency can and will intervene on their children's behalf. In short, many parents believe that disciplining kids has become illegal.

Although I deemed these common parental concerns almost totally erroneous, I contacted a State of Oregon Child Protective Services representative. I wanted a professional perspective on the legal rights and responsibilities of parents, especially as they relate to discipline and education.

Clare works as a CPS case manager. Her responsibilities include intervening in child abuse cases, placing children in foster care, terminating parental rights, and testifying in family courts about instances of abuse and neglect. I found her comments insightful and enlightening.

Together, let's take Clare's brief tour of parental rights and responsibilities from a Child Protective Services perspective.

Parental Responsibilities and Education

Legally, parents are responsible for assuring the State that their children attend school until the age when the children can legally drop out. Nowadays, in most states, juveniles must attend school until high school graduation or the age of eighteen. In a smaller number of states, the age of choice is sixteen or seventeen, but children can rarely drop out before age eighteen without parental consent. Attending school is the law.

Children must attend school unless they are sick—parents cannot simply decide to let a child stay home.

Parents are responsible for their child's behavior while at school, even if the parent is unaware of a child's misbehavior. Parents can be cited or sued if their children fail to attend school, if they harm someone at school, or if they break the law at school. This includes drug or alcohol use, truancy, theft, or threatening school staff or fellow students. Bullying is now a criminal offense in most states. Parents are expected, under law, to establish clear rules and regulations for their child, to be responsible for their child's behavior, and to monitor the child's conduct at school.

Parents are thus responsible for their child's behavior in the classroom and outside of school. The legal system assumes that children in the community are under the supervision of a legal guardian, usually the parents, and holds the legal guardian responsible for their children's conduct. Parents cannot legally allow their children to break any law, and that includes curfew laws, truancy statutes, liquor and tobacco laws pertaining to minors, substance abuse laws, and traffic regulations.

✵

Sara and I were introduced when I visited her at a school program in a residential treatment facility for unwed mothers. She was recovering from alcohol and drug abuse in preparation for having her first child. She was also trying to quit smoking. Sara was sixteen years old.

Prior to entering treatment, she lived with her mother and her mother's boyfriend in a small two-bedroom apartment. According to Sara, the adults were seldom home. When they were at home in the apartment, they often smoked and drank liquor. Sara's mother knew that Sara also smoked, and they split cartons of cigarettes that were purchased with the weekly groceries. They also shared six-packs of beer. Sara's mother's boyfriend and Sara were "good friends," and he frequently spent the night in the apartment. Sara's nineteen-year-old boyfriend also slept over frequently, with her mother's tacit approval.

Sara appreciated and defended her mother's permissiveness. "When she was sixteen, Mom did all the things I do, and she thinks they're OK for me, too. She's a good parent, and she wants me to be able to make my own decisions. She's not being irresponsible. She wants to treat me like an adult. If I make any bad decisions, they aren't my mother's fault, so I don't blame her."

I do blame Sara's mother. You can see the consequences of her irresponsibility and poor decisions: pregnancy, addiction, and a young girl's life in crisis. Her mother's decision to condone Sara's smoking and drinking was irresponsible and destructive, and also probably illegal in most states. Certainly, to allow Sara, a minor, to sleep with an older man, in her house, supported and encouraged her statutory rape. Thus, by acquiescence, Sara's mother became guilty of criminal behavior. Sara's mom assumed that Sara was capable of making adult decisions, but legally, it is the parent who is responsible. And, as evidence from Sara's life aptly demonstrates, putting this child in charge of decisions about sex, drugs, alcohol, and birth control was utter folly.

When parents abdicate their supervisory responsibilities, they become guilty of neglect. "How can I control my child's behavior," parents might ask, "when I can't discipline him or her, or when I'm not even there?" The answer is that parents also have definable rights pertaining to discipline.

◇

Parents' Rights

Parents have the right to establish rules of conduct for their children to follow. This includes setting a curfew and establishing study times.

Parents have the right to expect their children to follow home rules.

Parents may discipline their children *as they see fit,* unless the discipline harms the child or leads to neglect. Physically harming a child constitutes abuse, which is a form of assault. In most states, spanking is an allowed form of punishment, as long as it does not physically harm the child.

Parents have other sorts of rights. In the home, parents should feel, and be, safe from any and all threats of violence and actual violence. Their property and the property of the home should be safe and secure from harm or theft. Minors may not bring firearms, alcohol, tobacco,

explosives, or illegal drugs into the home. Parents have the right to con-
fiscate these substances, and anything else the parents deem unfit or
unhealthy for their children.

Parents have the right to insist that their children go to school and
participate in classes. They may contact the school and discuss the
child's performance without the child's consent. Parents can legally
access all confidential school records and all other records relating to
the child. The school cannot withhold records and academic information from parents, regardless of the minor child's wishes.

Legal Rights and Good Parenting

What these legal rights mean is that you have the right to be a good
parent, and the government is not going to arrest you or interfere with
you as you do your parenting job. You can establish rules, establish consequences, and enforce punishments. You can manage your own home
in a manner you think is most beneficial to your child's success and your
peace of mind.

I know of two instances where children have legally complained
about their parents and filed charges against them. I mentioned the case
involving Jackie and her daughters earlier in this book. I asked Clare
about such cases, which seemed to contradict her assertions about
parental rights. Here was Clare's response:

*"CPS workers are trained to distinguish casual complaints
from valid instances of child abuse. Actual, valid cases where chil-*

dren file charges against their parents are rare. Most of our cases involve blatant and severe abuse or neglect. They are reported by doctors, teachers, or other involved professionals. No one can assault or neglect their kids, but parents who simply want to manage their children's behavior have nothing to fear from Child Protective Services.

"In fact, a more serious problem in our office is that parents fail to provide their children enough structure. Parents get tired of the arguments, or feel that they cannot do anything about their kids' behavior, and they just give up. They don't want to get involved, or they're afraid of their children, or they're too busy.

"Many times, we at CPS see parents whose children are engaged in dangerous criminal activity, and the parents don't do a thing about it. That is neglect. When we confront parents about their kids' behavior, they say they can't do anything, but that's just not true. We wish that parents were more conscientious and took a greater interest in the progress and welfare of their children. We wish they would enforce rules—even call the police, if necessary. In fact, we give parenting classes that encourage parents to take charge and show some real leadership."

Clare continued by discussing the role of spanking, punishment, and discipline in a manner that closely coincides with some of the principles outlined in this book:

"It's true that you can spank your kids in most states, but I don't think it's the best strategy for dealing with kids. I was spanked frequently by my parents, and I didn't learn one thing from all those spankings. Most of our problems are with adolescents. Can you imagine spanking a teenage girl? I don't think it'll accomplish anything useful. Honestly, I think there are better ways

to control kids than spanking them.

"We encourage parents to establish home rules and conse-quences for misbehavior. We also suggest some rewards for doing a good job. Children dislike, more than anything else, when you take away access and privileges. Taking away phone privileges, or TV time, is much more effective than spanking or screaming. My own son hated it when we took away his phone for misbehaving. Screaming and arguing don't work because when everyone is shouting and arguing, emotions are running too hot for learning to happen. When parents use consequences, kids remember it and learn from it because the consequences take place when the child has time to think. It's not so personal, and it's not so violent."

Clare's comments make good sense, and they should certainly calm any parent's fears about the legality of managing their children's behavior. It is important to note Clare's argument that while parents may spank or similarly punish their children, it is usually not the best option. Establishing and enforcing consequences does the job just as well, and avoids many of the pitfalls associated with punishment, especially physical punishment. There *is* a better way.

In a wider context, parents who view themselves primarily as enforcers may be missing the boat. There is a great deal more to good parenting than enforcing the rules. Effective discipline and the management of consequences becomes effective only in the context of a larger program of good parenting, beginning with the attitudes and values that permeate the home and the parent-child relationship. This is where good parenting really begins.

The Foundations of Good Parenting

The bedrock of good parenting are the attitudes of caring and mutual regard. A solid parent-child relationship is built on respect, tolerance, and kindness. Most parents expect these attitudes from their children. Yet, they themselves often fail to demonstrate these attitudes when dealing with their children, their children's behavior, and their misbehavior. A few parents never learn how to treat their children with tolerance and respect. They are domineering, dictatorial, abrupt, and inflexible.

More often, though, I see parents who are open, caring, and respectful—until their youngsters do something wrong. Then, like Dr. Jeckyl and Mr. Hyde, the parent confronts the child like a madman. I've seen parents throw tantrums, kick furniture, toss objects, break dishes, jump up and down, shake, cry, and scream. Yet, if a child becomes angry and acts out, the same parents are convinced that they have spawned a monster. Keeping in mind that our children learn from our behavior, think about this truism:

When your children get angry, they are probably going to act like you do when you get angry.

Now, that's a grim thought, isn't it?

Anger and frustration are natural emotions. Even if you are the world's best parent, you are going to get angry and frustrated sometimes. That is part and parcel of the parenting job. But, when your emotions are in full swing, it is important to manage your anger, and channel it into constructive ends. Exploding doesn't accomplish anything except alien-

97

ate your children. And, when your children become irate and explosive, it bears asking: Where does that behavior originate? When we manage our own anger, we teach our children to manage theirs.

For parents dealing with misbehavior, the key ingredients to successfully resolving disputes are respect, tolerance, and kindness. Learn to express your anger honestly and openly. Explain why you feel you were wronged. Establish a consequence for the wrongdoing. But don't express anger by threats and screaming. Emphasize the behavior, not the child. Sit down and speak calmly. Avoid name-calling. In short, act exactly how you would like your child to act in the next dispute—calmly and reasonably.

Try to develop a relationship with your children that is based on more than authority. A caring attitude and a positive relationship with your children will always carry more weight than the power of your authority. Behavior management should take place within the larger context of a loving relationship based on affection and kindness, openly expressed and mutually appreciated.

Parents who get along well with their kids have few problems when disciplining them. Parents who don't bother to build a solid relationship with their children are hard-pressed when dealing with misbehavior. Power is a shallow basis for attempting to manage behavior. Love, respect, and discipline are not mutually exclusive. They are the foundations of good parenting.

Change is not a power play. Love, respect, and discipline are the keys to successful change.

CHAPTER EIGHT

School is a Full-Time Job

---

*If you cry "forward," you must be sure to make clear
the direction in which to go. Don't you see that if you fail to
do that, and simply call out the word to a monk and a revolutionary,
they will go in precisely opposite directions?*
—Anton Chekhov

This chapter may be the hardest of all for you to accept and will require the most courage for you to implement. As I previously warned, when your child catches wind of your plans to really start changing things, he or she will hit the roof. You will have to anticipate conflict and prepare to manage it. You will have to say "no" repeatedly. So, before we begin with the specifics of organizational planning, let's arm you against the eventuality of resistance and backlash from your youngster.

The Policeman Model

Traffic police are expertly and extensively trained on how to handle the enforcement of policies and rules. When someone is stopped, say, for speeding, the officer greets the driver, asks for ID and paperwork, notes the driver's speed and the speed limit, and issues a citation. Pretty straightforward, isn't it?

Let's discuss what the officer does *not* do. The officer does not shout or lose his temper. He does not jump up and down, call the driver stupid or lazy, or threaten him with a beating. He does not cry or pout or play the victim. He does not throw things or kick the car. He does not debate the fairness of the speed limit. He is not concerned if the driver is angry or not. He does not care if the driver blames Mom or whines about a hard life. The cop takes it all in stride and just enforces the rules. The gist of the conversation is always something like this:

"Hi there! Beautiful morning, isn't it? I stopped you because the speed limit here is 55 mph. You were doing 80 mph. Here's the ticket. Drive carefully. Have a nice day."

Here is an ideal role model for parents to follow when enforcing rules, expectations, and discipline! Some specific details of the policeman's routine are worth noting:

- Once an infraction is detected, do not debate the rule or its fairness.

- Don't argue. State the rule that's been violated, the fact that it has been violated, and what the consequences are.

- Don't state the issue in personal terms, like how the infraction affects you personally—you are just an administrator doing your job.

- If someone gets angry, that's his or her problem.

- Never accept excuses, blaming, tall tales, whining, or pleadings for "another chance." If someone breaks the rule, the consequences follow. Period.

If it sounds simple, it is. But, it may not be easy to implement. Old habits die hard, and you can easily get sucked into an argument, shouting match, pouting session, or debate. Why bother, though? Haven't you argued enough? Has it done you any good? Believe it or not, the policeman's approach works better, if you only follow one simple but inflexible rule:

Enforcement must be consistent and unvarying.

Once you start enforcing the rules, you need to do so without exception, without flexibility, and without recourse to discussion. If your children see that you may not mean business, that any of their old tricks may still work, you will be back to the same old nonsense.

When your children blow up about the new plan—and they may— your best response is to just let them vent, and then say, "When you're done, let's discuss the details, because this is the way it's going to be." Your children's anger will pass, and you will maintain your dignity, authority, and peace of mind.

This is not to suggest that parents should never be caring and affectionate. But, mixing feelings and discipline can send false signals and allow for emotions to overshadow the point of the discipline. It is the negative emotionalism surrounding discipline that leads to arguments, shouting, threats, and tantrums. Try instead to focus impersonally on the issues and consequences as if you were an administrator doing a necessary, albeit unpleasant, job.

Your child's initial anger will probably be followed by a campaign of passive aggression and withdrawal of affection. But, you have learned that you do not have to buy into this antagonism. You do not need to pester, threaten, or argue. You can acknowledge to yourself that this juvenile behavior is a manipulative ploy, plain and simple, and not take it personally. Then, like a well-trained traffic police officer, you can simply administer the established laws of your home, in an impersonal manner, allowing your child to react as he or she may react.

Remember that you are doing this for your child and his or her future. More importantly, you are doing it for yourself. You have the right to raise your kids as you see fit. You have the right to have certain expectations. You have the right to expect a peaceful home and peace of mind.

Your child, on the other hand, has no right to deprive you of these things because of rebelliousness, stubbornness, or laziness. Instead of sticking up for your child, isn't it time to stick up for yourself?

Yet, there is more to this than selfishly acting in your own behalf. Your children need to learn that they are not at the center of the universe, and that their covert aggression and temper tantrums are not acceptable in an adult world. They must come to realize that if they want to be treated as adults, they must act like adults. As parents, we must help them grow up, even if they do not always like it. Allowing them to capitalize upon their immature behavior does no one any good.

A Primer on Payoffs

The transition to responsible adulthood requires that kids learn some difficult and valuable lessons about work and responsibility. These lessons are part of the culture of success. In the transition to responsible adulthood, one difficult lesson is that we must accept life's responsibilities in order to reap life's rewards. There is no free lunch.

✷

I suffer from seasonal allergies. Some early May mornings, my eyes are so bleary and my nose so swollen that I wonder if I'll make it through the workday. Exhausted from a restless night, I feel absolutely terrible. "It would be so great," I ponder dreamily, "to take the day off and just rest at home." I hit the snooze button and drift off into a fantasy about calling in sick . . . but, since I am a responsible adult, I snap out of it, sit up muttering, and stumble out of bed for hot tea and a decongestant tablet. Work, of course, waits for no man—and I've got to go.

We adults know that, unless we are exceedingly wealthy, going to work is a necessity of modern life. We may or may not enjoy our jobs, but we go because we need the things the world of work provides. Work brings home the bacon—it also pays the rent, puts gas in the car, and clothes the kids. We may not like the idea of going to work on a cold morning, but we like and need to get paid. We do it because there is a payoff.

You don't need to be a psychologist to understand an important fundamental principle of human behavior:

People do things because there is a payoff.

Conversely, people will not do things when they see no payoff forthcoming. The payoff may not necessarily be monetary or even materialistic. A philanthropist, for example, may donate money to a charity simply for the pleasure of feeling altruistic and acting benevolently. But, the payoff is always there, even for the philanthropist.

Let's apply this simple principle to your child's behavior and ask some not-so-simple questions:

- Why should your child want to do well in school? Where is the payoff?

- Is there a payoff for not working hard in school?

- If all of your child's wants and needs are satisfied, and your child is content and comfortable, why should he or she change?

- What is the payoff for your child's behavior right now? By behaving in a certain way at school, what is he or she getting out of it?

One of the first things many new lottery winners do is quit their jobs. Once their motivation for working is eliminated, once work no longer provides them a payoff, they have no further interest in the world of work. Similarly, your child has no reason to work in school unless there are rewards for doing well and consequences for not achieving. As things stand, there are many natural payoffs for *not* performing in school:

- Your child has more free time for recreation.

- Your child gets to avoid a great deal of responsibility.

- Your child is able to blame others for his failure to act responsibly.

- Your child can buck authority and get away with it.

- Your child can avoid doing hard work.

There must be a payoff for doing well at school. Somehow, you must see to it that the payoffs are greater for achieving than for under-performing, and that the negative consequences for poor grades are greater, too.

Some parents simply bribe their kids to do well, offering money, prizes, or special rewards for good grades. The danger of this approach is that it pays children to do what they should do anyway—act respon-sibly. Children who are paid off for acting responsibly learn a sense of entitlement, and their parents fall into the common traps of giving in to keep the peace, trying to buy affection, and not accepting their respon-sibility to work for change.

⚏

Randy and Bobby were identical, fiercely competitive seven-year-old twins. They insisted that whenever one received some-thing, the other must get it, too. Unfortunately, their parents chronically referred to them in the plural as "the twins," and the parents bought into the idea that they should treat them "equally" in all respects.

Both Randy and Bobby were thumb suckers, and classmates teased them about their habit. The boys' parents agreed to pay each of them $20.00 a month for a year if they would finally give up the thumb sucking.

The scheme worked well for about a month, and Randy and Bobby needed few reminders to keep their thumbs out of their mouths. But after awhile, Bobby began the habit again, especially in front of the TV, where all the family could watch him violate his end of the bargain. Randy complained that it was unfair to pay Bobby $20.00 a month when he had started sucking again, and the parents agreed to quit paying Bobby. Then, Bobby became angry and jealous because Randy was getting $20.00 a month and he *wasn't. According to Bobby, "I can't help it. You should all leave me alone and quick picking on me. You always give Randy extra stuff and then make excuses for him."*

What a mess! You could fault Bobby for generalizing unfairly, playing the victim, blaming his parents, and feeling entitled. But, underneath it all, the parents were at fault for cooking up the whole scheme in the first place. Money is not a natural consequence of thumb sucking—it is a bribe, pure and simple. The twins' parents never should have paid them to do what should have been expected of them anyway. If they had allowed natural consequences to take their course, the ribbing the twins were receiving at school would have eventually put an end to the problem.

◆

Bribes, Payments, and Rewards

Parents need to confront their children and challenge them to accept responsibility. Part of good parenting is to teach children that accepting responsibility is part and parcel of growing up, even when an immediate reward is not apparent. This may seem straightforward, yet doesn't teaching kids to accept responsibilities without being paid contradict the principle of performing for payoffs? The confusion surrounding children and payoffs is greatly simplified if we distinguish between bribes, payments, and rewards.

A bribe is coercive. When we bribe children, we give them money or goods to do something they should do anyway. Paying Randy and Bobby to stop thumb sucking is a good example of a bribe, because they were paid for behavior that should have been expected. Bribing is destructive because youngsters do not learn to accept responsibility.

Bribing children to do what is expected of them, or paying them to accept their responsibilities, is problematic because they will learn not to perform the task without the bribe. This is what happened with my Silent Sustained Reading group at the children's home. After they were paid to read, they would not read without the bribe. Somewhere, the notion that children should read, for the sheer enjoyment of it, got lost in the negotiations. Bribed children learn to accept responsibility only when they are paid for it. This is destructive because accepting responsibility is a key factor in achieving academic success. It is also a key step in the process of emotional maturation.

A payment, on the other hand, suggests a business relationship— payment rendered for services performed. Payment occurs when someone completes an agreed upon service for an agreed upon price. For example, my father paid me ten cents a window each fall to wash the insides of our storm windows in preparation for winter. It was not a normal duty, and I did not get paid until I did it. The job and the price were agreed upon beforehand. We had a business deal. Payments are a sensible means of teaching children about responsibility and the world of adult work, as long as payments are used on a contract basis—payment for services rendered—and not as a means to coerce normal, responsible behavior.

A reward is earned for doing something exceptional—above and beyond the call of duty. People earn rewards for exceptional behavior. For example, many parents pay their children a reward for good grades. These payments are typically for *high* marks—it would be foolish to pay your child a reward for D's and F's! The intent of rewards is to promote excellence over mediocrity (or failure). We reward our children to encourage them to excel. Rewards are a powerful and effective means to encourage excellence—if they are used *only* for outstanding work or behavior. When you distribute rewards for mundane performance, you encourage mediocrity.

Admittedly, the distinctions between bribes, payments, and rewards may, in actual practice, be blurry, so it is important to clarify to your child *why* they are getting the rewards you give them. You must rigorously limit rewards to encourage exceptional performance. Rewards are most effective when combined with a solid program of logical consequences for bad behavior.

◈

Confronting Your Child About Bad Grades

Before you begin this difficult discussion, let me remind you of three points that may help harden your resolve:

- Whatever you have been doing about grades, it has not been working. The grades are still terrible.

- Whatever your child has been doing isn't working, either. The grades are still terrible.

- If you are tired of the awful grades, you and your child are going to have to do something different.

Eventually, you are going to have to confront your child about grades. How you do this is vitally important. Limit the discussion to grades and your desire that your child improve them. This is not the time to argue about other issues or to make sweeping, general comments about your youngster's behavior. Do not mix school goals and other sorts of goals. Stick to the grades.

Try to remove emotions from the discussion. Do not blame, accuse, threaten, or argue. Stress repeatedly that you are not angry, and that this is not a fight. You simply need and want to tell the child to do something to get the grades up. It is important to clearly stress to your child that,

He or she has a job—school—and school is a full-time job.

There is nothing that takes priority over doing well in school. As soon as you and your child both accept this, decisions about a course of action will begin to make sense.

Here are some points to ponder before confronting your child:

- Plan ahead for this discussion. Set up a time with your youngster. Don't try to catch him or her as he or she goes out the door. Prepare your behavioral objectives beforehand.

- Don't waffle on the issue. Explain candidly that you need to discuss bad grades and what you two are going to do about them.

- Expect some anger from your child. Remembering our analogy of the policeman, ignore the anger. Keep to the business at hand.

- Limit the discussion. Even if your child begins to drift into other areas, focus the discussion back onto grades and school.

- Stress repeatedly that you are not trying to control your child or to punish him or her in any way. The only objective is improved grades.

- Use specific language to discuss the problem. Avoid words

like "never" and "always" and avoid accusations. "I am concerned that you are failing both English and Biology," is better than, "You always do a bad job in school."

- State your goals for your child's future behavior. One or two goals are plenty. Be sure that the goals are modest and reasonable, and that they are not subject to broad interpretation.

- Set a timeline, allowing for the time it will take to bring grades up. A good goal might be,

**Beginning no more than 30 days from now,
you will maintain a "C" average or better in all your classes.**

- Allow a grace period, like 30 days, and explain that you are willing to offer advice, encouragement, and help. Express your confidence that your child will take the discussion to heart and bring the grades up.

- Discuss the idea that you have a job at work, and that doing the job right is your responsibility as an adult. Your child has a full-time job as well. That job is being a student. That job, too, has to be done right.

- Note that after the probationary period, there will be consequences if the grades do not improve to the stated goal. Explain that this is not a punishment. It is merely a strategy for keeping distractions away from your child while pursuing the full-time job of being a student.

- Make your child responsible for what happens. When the grades meet the set goals, he will be in charge of managing his own affairs. When the grades fall outside the objectives, you will have to take over. Stress that he can control what he wants to happen by controlling his grades.

You may want to consider planning out your discussion and what you want to say beforehand. Your text need not be written out, but it might look and sound something like this:

"I have a job. I go to work every day because my job affords us the things we need. Our house, car, clothes, and bills are all paid for by the money I make from working. If I don't work, we no longer get these necessities. I have a choice—I can go and do a good job, I can go and do a less than good job, or I can stay home. I choose to go and do a good job, in part because my job gives us the things we want and need.

"I have a boss. My boss is in charge of making sure that my work gets done and done right. He helps me do a good job, but he also tells me when I'm doing something wrong. That's his responsibility. If I'm doing something wrong, or my work isn't as good as it could be, my supervisor lets me know.

"Your full-time job is going to school. It's the most important job you have. It comes before dating, friends, work, sports, or recreation. It's important that you do well in school, because your full-time job as a student helps you learn the things that you'll need later on in life.

"Right now, you aren't doing your job well. And, like my job, if you aren't doing well, you aren't going to get the things you want any more. I'm your supervisor, and it's my job to let you know that you need to do better. I'll help you in any way I can, because it's my responsibility to be sure you do a good job as a student."

Explain to your child that you are going to help him or her get organized. Point out that you and the teacher have gotten together and formed a partnership (*forming a home-school alliance is the subject of*

111

Chapter 10), and thus will cooperate with you. Establish a grace period and set a deadline for progress. If the grades are up by then, you will continue to help in any way you can. But, if performance has not improved by then, you are going to have to impose a plan of action, just like any responsible supervisor would. After all, the work must get done right.

✠

As a student, Scott was a walking disaster. A sixth-grade son of missionaries, he attended a South American international school where I taught. Scott often accompanied his parents on their missionary trips into the Andes Mountains. He loved working with the poor people there, and he was hard-working and responsible. But, in the city, he did little, if any, schoolwork and was constantly in trouble for various minor infractions of school rules. He misplaced books, lost homework, arrived to class late, fell asleep in classes, and turned in the wrong assignments. His desk and locker were a mess. Scott was an outgoing and likeable kid—he just couldn't seem to organize himself, settle down, and get busy at school.

I called in Scott's parents. They freely admitted that, although they were concerned, they were also extremely involved in their missionary work, and, as a result, had failed to pay enough attention to Scott's studies. They didn't know what to do to bring Scott's grades up, but they were willing to listen and to try anything. We agreed to form a plan of action and then to confront Scott together.

When we met with Scott, I explained "our" concerns about his grades and school behavior. Then, his mother recounted Scott's fine contribution to their missionary work. She explained that what he did in the city, at school, was just as important to him and to the family. She indicated that his poor school performance was inter-

fering with their missionary activity because the family could ill-afford to leave for work in the mountains when Scott was behind at school. And, all things considered, school came first.

We discussed the meaning of the family's work and Scott's responsibility to pitch in and do his fair share by maintaining acceptable grades. He seemed to understand, and his grades improved dramatically for a few weeks. Then, it was back to the old story of lower marks and misbehavior.

Fortunately, I had told Scott's parents to expect setbacks and they were committed for the long haul. We began to have weekly conferences with Scott about his grades. We encouraged, we praised, we criticized, and we established clear consequences for setbacks. We reminded Scott that his primary job was school and we expected him to do it well. We made him responsible on a daily basis. We asked for his help. We demanded his compliance.

Scott never did become an outstanding student, but his grades came up and his misbehavior went down. The grades were important, but what is most pleasing about Scott's story is that he learned to be responsible and accept his part in managing his own affairs. Our real victory was not just academic. We helped Scott down the path to maturity and adulthood. He grew up—and probably more than a little.

Establishing Natural Consequences

The best consequences for behavior are natural ones. As a child, for example, you learn not to put your hand on hot objects, because the natural consequences are quick and apparent.

The natural consequences for poor school performance are financial, social, and career disadvantages in adulthood. Yet, as you recall,
such future penalties—because they are not immediately felt—are inef-
fective in controlling the behavior of children because kids have a hard
time projecting into an abstract future. You are going to have to build
immediate consequences into your child's life to counteract poor academic performance. When establishing consequences for behavior,
there is one great principle you should follow:

Punishments punish, but good consequences teach.

The most obvious and effective consequences are those that logically follow from behavior. Imposed consequences are never as good as
those that naturally occur, but prescribed consequences that make sense
and follow logically from the unacceptable behavior still work well.

❁

*In my parenting classes, I always encourage parents to bring
their kids along to class. Once, Marv and his son, Patrick, were
attending my class on consequences. Patrick had been caught
throwing eggs at an unpopular neighbor's pickup truck and
camper, and Marv had decided that they should discuss an appropriate punishment during our class time.*

*My first idea was for Patrick to clean the truck, but the neigh-
bor had already done that. So, we discussed what the natural consequences had been for Marv's neighbor. The neighbor had been
forced to go out on a cold winter morning and clean frozen eggs off
his truck. He had been inconvenienced, angered, and put through
the uncomfortable experience of having to complain to Marv*

about Patrick's behavior.

Marv had suffered consequences, too. He had to deal with an embarrassed and irate neighbor, and felt the obvious need to apologize for something he had not done. We decided that the real issue was not the eggs, but the inconvenience and embarrassment that Patrick had caused his father and his neighbor.

We decided that Patrick should provide a custom cleaning and detailing of the interior and exterior of his neighbor's camper and pickup. We also decided that Patrick, alone, needed to discuss with his neighbor the whole affair, offer an apology, and arrange a time for the detailing. This would allow Patrick to experience firsthand the kind of social discomfort that arises from these sorts of situations.

The consequences that followed from Patrick's misbehavior were logical and obvious. He had harmed the pickup and his neighbor, and he had to make up for the natural inconvenience his neighbor experienced because of the misbehavior. Patrick's egg throwing had also caused his father a great deal of embarrassment, and we wanted Patrick to experience that social discomfort himself.

Patrick's father could have grounded him or taken away certain privileges, but those *punishments* would not have let Patrick see the cause-and-effect relationship between his behavior and its consequences.

I fondly remember Patrick's story because it had an unexpectedly happy ending. Patrick's neighbor, Mr. Crotke, gave him a merciless ribbing, and then showed Patrick into his garage. Inside was a well-equipped repair bay, and Mr. Crotke invited Patrick and his friends over any time they wanted to work on cars. A fast friendship developed. Soon

Mr. Crotke, who had previously been an isolated and unpopular neighbor, became known and liked by all the local teens, and his garage became the after-school home for several of the neighbors' boys.

Now that you understand how to devise consequences that teach instead of punishments that simply punish, let's see how this principle plays out in a more sophisticated example:

Sandy, an adolescent behavioral client of mine, lived with her recently divorced mother, Veronica, who had been awarded custody of Sandy. Her husband had weekend visitation rights. I had been working with Sandy for some time and watched her go through her parents' break-up. I quickly noticed that Sandy had become an expert at playing one parent off against the other to extort clothes, money, property, and privileges from both.

Sandy's father had fallen into the parenting trap of trying to buy her affection, and her weekend visits with him routinely entailed a shopping spree at the mall. She usually came home with new clothes, make-up, and other things her father had purchased for her during her weekend visit.

Veronica, on the other hand, was a strict disciplinarian, prone to anger and threats. After fights with her mother, Sandy would often stomp off to her father's and refuse to come home. Finally, after an argument about dating a certain boy, Sandy did not come home for several days. Veronica received a call from her ex-husband's attorney, who explained that Sandy had decided to live with her dad. Would Veronica agree to a reversal of the custody terms, with her father given custody and Veronica receiving visitation rights? Fed up and deeply hurt by her daughter's manipulation, Veronica capitulated, and begrudgingly agreed to twice-

monthly visits and her payment of substantial child support payments.

When Sandy arrived for her first visit, she quickly thanked her mom for "giving in and letting me live with Dad," and then began to explain her agenda for the weekend. She had certain things she needed for school—she was out of shampoo, deodorant, and hygiene products—and she wanted to buy some new shoes. She also announced that she had a weekend date with her boyfriend. Veronica countered, "No, I am not going to do your shopping for you. I pay your father a lot of money to support you, and he needs to buy you your things. And, I told you I would not allow you to go out with that boy. I don't care what your father lets you do, but you can't go out with him while you're staying with me." Sandy, furious at her mother's flat rebuff, refused to stay, and Veronica took her back home to her father.

A few weeks later, Sandy called again and wanted to come over. This time, Sandy stayed the weekend and complained that she was not happy with her father. Apparently, he was now no more understanding of her demands than Veronica was, and Sandy had gotten angry and stormed out. When Sunday afternoon rolled around, Sandy did not want to go home and asked Veronica if she could stay a few days until "Dad quits being so mean to me." "No, Sandy," Veronica carefully explained. "You decided to go live with your father. You have school tomorrow. Moving in with him was your choice, and he is responsible for you now. You have to go home."

Veronica was right to put her foot down—many parents never do. When Veronica recounted this story, she told me it had been very hard for her to say "no" to her daughter. Yet, she explained that she did not want to teach Sandy the wrong lessons by allowing her to continue to manipulate the situation. Instead, said Veronica, she wanted Sandy to understand that there were consequences for her actions and that she had to learn to live with them.

Veronica's and Sandy's problems were never completely resolved. Sandy continued to attempt to manipulate Veronica, and continually tried to exploit her for cash and purchases. Part of the problem was that Veronica's ex-husband tried to compete against Veronica for Sandy's affection and constantly subverted her parental authority. Sandy could never see that things had really changed with her mother. She kept trying the same old stuff, hoping that Veronica would finally cave in.

But, Veronica did what was right for her. She liberated herself from the stress and anxiety of putting up with Sandy's nonsense. She quit being an emotional hostage, and began to manage her life in her own best interests. She faced her fears, accepted her responsibilities as a parent, and did the right thing. She made Sandy live up to the natural consequences of her actions.

Teaching the right lessons by establishing consequences instead of imposing punishments is exactly the attitude you must adopt when dealing with your youngster's bad grades. Let's see if we can devise some consequences that teach instead of punish. First, a few reminders about bad grades and school are in order:

- If things are going to get better, the grades must come first.

- School is your child's full-time job.

- Anything that is interfering with or distracting from schoolwork, or using up time that should be dedicated to it, must go.

- Your child is going to need an enforced study time until grades improve.

- Unless your child can take the responsibility for changing things around, you are going to have to take charge and reorganize your child's work skills and habits.

Ask yourself what activities in your youngster's life are taking time away from studies:

- Does your child watch too much TV?

- Is your child constantly on the computer?

- Is your child at home long enough to get anything done?

- Is your child's after-school job or sports practice getting in the way?

- Is your child's primary problem motivational or organizational?

- Is your child simply too busy with other stuff?

Take an inventory of your child's behavior and set some priorities about what you will most need to control. Consider what your child's payoffs are for not doing well. Make sure that whatever consequences you choose, they are directly related to what seems to be interfering with getting better grades.

Some Suggestions for Consequences

No one can tell you what consequences will be most appropriate for your youngster. Younger children, of course, will need different consequences than older teens, and each child is unique.

A daughter may be ignoring school because she is spending too much time with a boyfriend. A son may be distracted from homework by his computer or video games. But, keeping in mind that we want to take away the payoffs for poor performance and help kids avoid the things that keep them from their studies, here are some general suggestions to help you get started. Remember, select consequences that are naturally apparent in your child's life. Don't just use this list as "the best" consequences to apply:

- Establish a nightly study time and adhere to it invariably.

- Schedule time, each morning and evening, to discuss school with your child. Ask pointed questions and examine schoolwork.

- Cut back on the activities where your child spends the most time, especially activities that limit study time. (Do you remember Brad, the brilliant computer geek who was not completing his schoolwork? We decided to limit his computer access until his homework was completed and checked. He became quite angry, but his grades improved.)

- Don't fix what isn't broken. If your child is excelling in a positive activity, don't limit that activity. Try to cut back on things that waste time and accomplish little, like TV, phone conversations, and computer use.

- Limit activities that seem to interfere with schoolwork. Sports, romances, friendships, and jobs are all laudable pursuits, but they cannot be allowed to interfere with school.

- Don't let kids engage in leisure activity until schoolwork is done. Don't allow "couch potato" pursuits like computer games, naps, phone conversations, TV, or other sedentary activities until the work is complete, checked, and in the backpack.

Your child will probably want to argue about these restrictions on their freedom and independence. Don't be drawn in. Explain that you are not trying to blame or punish. Merely point out that these activities seem to be interfering with academics, and they have to be restricted until the grades come up. Your youngster is free to enjoy his pursuits and hobbies—*after* the work is done, and done well.

Your child can have more control over how he spends his time when he can reach the modest goals that you have established. While he is within the parameters of your academic objectives, he is in control of his life. When he falls below the minimum standards, you must take over. His job as a student is to do well in school—your job as a parent is to ensure that he does. Be sure to note that you are giving him a grace period as a chance to improve before you are forced to apply consequences.

The Grace Period

A grace period is fair and necessary. It will allow both of you to become accustomed to the idea that you are taking charge. It will allow your child to adjust to new schedules and demands. And it will let you see if your youngster is capable of managing his or her own school affairs. Many children turn around at this juncture, making the imposition of sanctions unnecessary.

⬧

Marie was a vivacious seventeen-year-old girl who was enjoying all the benefits of a full adolescent life. She dated several boys, drove a late-model sports car, and worked after school at a restaurant to make her car payments, buy clothes, and pursue her various social activities. She enjoyed cross-country mountain bike racing on weekends and took aerobics classes at a nearby gym. Gregarious and outgoing, Marie was seldom at home, and her grades began to suffer.

Marie's parents were aspiring to a professional career for her and investigating colleges when they began to panic about her grades. They discussed the problem, contacted me, and decided to form a plan of action. They invited Marie out to dinner and confronted her with the contradiction between her career aspirations—she, too, expected to become a professional—and her academic performance. They explained that they were not angry and did not want to punish or blame her. As parents, they simply needed her grades to come up. Marie could either handle it, or Mom and Dad would intervene.

Marie's parents explained that she had until the end of the marking period to bring her grades up to a 3.0 average, and to have nothing lower than a "C" in all classes. They would support her efforts and help in any way they could. They also wanted to examine her homework, check her assignments daily, and expected her home by 10:00 p.m. each school night. They noted that they had already arranged various parent-teacher conferences and had enlisted her teachers' support. But, if Marie could not meet the new objectives at school, she would have to begin nightly study hours, forcing her to quit her evening job and limiting her other activities.

Happily, Marie saw the wisdom of buckling down and working to improve her grades. She was able to responsibly manage her time and juggle her schedule to allow for study and homework time, and her grades improved. Her parents continued to monitor her progress and check her work daily, and insisted that she be home at 10:00 each school night. They contacted her teachers on a regular basis and reported their discussions to Marie. But Marie took charge and accepted responsibility for her schoolwork, so additional consequences proved unnecessary.

❖

Monitoring Your Child's Progress

If you are going to assure yourself that your child is doing his work and is making some progress towards set goals, you are going to have to devise some plan to accurately monitor progress. There are several different ways you can get information about how things are going at school. Many of these strategies may already be in place:

- Keep in close contact with teachers. Remember that they are quite jealous of their time. Try for quick but frequent progress checks. Teachers like checklists, because they do not have to write out time-consuming details.

- Try to get a sense of your child's daily schedule and what goes on during the school day.

- Tell your child that you want to see *everything* that comes back from the teacher, graded or not. Get a folder and save all of it.

- During your organizational conference with your child each morning, find out what is going to happen at school that day. Get specifics. Ask pointed questions. You may want to take notes so you can refer to them during later conferences with your child and during exchanges with teachers.

- Check homework, folders, and the backpack on a daily basis. Look over everything that goes to school, even if you do not entirely understand the content.

- Assign your child the responsibility of demonstrating progress. Inform your child that, if he wants to continue to be in charge and avoid consequences, he is going to have to show you that he has improved.

- Discuss your child's progress with him regularly. Your child must know that you are monitoring his performance on a daily basis. Maintain a dialogue about school and grades.

- Praise accomplishments. Every sign of progress is a cause for celebration. Make sure your child knows that you are genuinely thrilled by each success. After all, isn't that what you are really after?

Unfortunately, when grades improve, it is easy for you to become complacent, assuming that the problem has been solved forever. Continue to monitor progress, maintain close communication with the school, and examine completed work.

It is easy for your child, too, to slip back into old habits. Your help in setting standards, maintaining vigilance, and checking progress will help your child maintain the academic performance you have both worked so hard to attain.

CHAPTER NINE

Getting Down to Business at Home

If you want to make enemies, try to change something.
—Woodrow Wilson

This chapter is about reorganizing your child's life. It will explain how the simple reorganizing of things can promote a great deal of school progress. As you read the instructions for organizing space and managing time and information, be sure to implement the steps immediately. Reading about change does no good—it is the action that brings results. Try to discuss proposed changes and their reasons with your child and your family. Enlist support and cooperation.

If you are faced with apathy and indifference, start the program of change anyway. Remember that apathy and passive aggression are cunning and insidious enemies—you defeat them by facing your fears and moving forward.

Reorganizing the Home Front

Having discussed the police officer's (and now the parent's) approach to enforcement, let's get down to some details about rearranging and reorganizing the home environment of your child. We'll pay special attention to how your child's study environment is organized, but you may be asked to make some uncomfortable changes in your schedule and habits as well. Try to remember the first principle, that *if nothing changes, nothing changes,* and realize that these difficult changes have been a long time coming.

It is important to first set the stage in your child's mind. Schedule a time to discuss the problem without interruption. Do not tack the conversation onto an argument about grades. Open the discussion by stating that your child is not in trouble and that you are not angry. Nor are you trying to blame anybody. The changes that are going to happen are not a punishment or a penalty—you simply need to do something to get the child's grades back on track. Talking and arguing have not worked, and it is time for you, as the responsible parent, to make sure your child gets educated. You are going to do whatever it takes to ensure your child's academic success.

If you want some insights into the organizational problems of young people, look in their rooms. The awful, cluttered mess of most kids' bedrooms is probably a good indication of how they organize their schoolwork and manage their academic lives. Students may have all the information, but their mental, physical, and organizational bad habits keep them from retrieving what they know and presenting it in a cogent fashion. When you add a cluttered desk in an untidy room to a disorganized binder in a messy backpack full of mixed-up supplies and books, then toss in an unorganized, cluttered mind for added measure, is it any wonder that some students cannot manage in school? Organization is such an important key to school survival, several good books have been written on this subject alone.

Here are some ways to organize and manage your child's academic life at home:

The Study Area: Find one study area and stick to it. It needs to be a place where your child can work alone, away from siblings, noise, and traffic. Make sure it is clean, organized, comfortable, and equipped with all the pens, pencils, paper, and other essentials needed for schoolwork. Be sure that the area is free from distractions like phones, games, electronic gadgets, magazines, toys, and anything else that may derail an easily distracted youngster. This includes the TV and probably the computer. A stereo may be acceptable if the music is low and calming—many kids can't stand absolute quiet and need background noise to concentrate. Booming headphones, however, won't cut it.

The Schedule: Decide on a study schedule and stick to it without exception. At the beginning, until grades improve, study time should be Sunday through Thursday evenings at a time when you can supervise what your child is doing. During study time, phone calls cannot be accepted, visitors will have to leave, and the TV must stay off. The study room door should stay open so you can periodically assure yourself that the work session is still in full swing. The family will have to hold down noise and eliminate distractions. Everyone, including your spouse, will have to understand that your child must be left alone to study.

During study time, encourage frequent breaks. Have snacks and drinks available. High school kids should break 10 minutes each hour. Younger children may need to rest every 20 minutes or so. Make sure breaks are brief and that your child then gets back to work. Try to get an estimate from the teacher about the quantity of homework your child is assigned, and how long it should take, and plan some time each night for going over homework.

Bedtime is an important consideration. Children need at least ten hours of sleep nightly. Adolescents should have a minimum of eight.

Mornings are important, too. Rushing is counterproductive in the morning, when your child has organizational tasks to accomplish. Figure on about 45-60 minutes each morning to get ready, and then, working backwards, assign a specific bedtime. Research suggests that lack of sleep is a major contributing factor to children's poor grades and behavior problems. Make sure your child is well-rested and has plenty of time each morning to eat a nutritional breakfast and carefully prepare for the school day to come.

Recreational reading contributes to many of the skills that promote learning at school. Bedtime is a great time for silent recreational reading. Once bedtime is set, allow your child to read in bed for awhile. A 15-30 minute reading period will help your child settle down and rest before sleeping, and might attract him or her to the world of books. Find out what kinds of reading materials your youngster enjoys and make them readily available. Teen magazines, comics, science fiction, and romance novels might all be appropriate. During recreational reading time, content is not as important as practice or the habits that daily reading encourages. Make sure, however, that this is quiet time, not time used for watching TV or listening to music. If your children do not want to read, they can turn off the light and go to sleep.

Mornings are often neglected as a key part of the school routine, resulting in forgotten books and assignments, temper tantrums, disorganization, and a general lack of preparedness for the school day. Because many families rush through the morning, their kids arrive at school keyed up and stressed out. Do you recall Matt, my dyslexic nephew whom I told you about in Chapter 5? I once spent a few days visiting his family, and no TV sitcom could compare to the mayhem and utter chaos of Matt's home in the early morning.

-⊄⊅-

I knew it was time to wake up because of the noise. Booming stereos in three teens' bedrooms added to the racket of a morning news program blaring out of the living room TV. Above the din, Matt's mother was shouting up the stairs to his father, reminding him to pick up dinner after work. At 7:00 a.m., Matt's home sounded like Grand Central Station at rush hour.

I stumbled down the stairs for coffee, and all five family members were standing around the kitchen table, shoveling down breakfast in a frenzy. Under the table, two large and excited dogs barked, mooched food, wagged tails, and generally added to the confusion. Matt's mother was issuing directives and reminders to everyone. His father was arguing with Matt's older brother about a dent in the Jeep. His sister was chatting about her work schedule to, it seemed, no one in particular. And Matt was on the phone with a friend, trying to clear up a question about the previous night's homework assignment, while he also packed up books and papers strewn among the breakfast dishes. Matt was "preparing" for the school day ahead.

Can you imagine Matt's state of mind as he left home for classes? It is no wonder he struggled at school with organization and time management. His madhouse morning doomed him from the beginning of each day.

Organize the morning routine. Take time each morning to eat a solid breakfast with your child and discuss the school day ahead. Make this morning school conference a daily routine. Go over homework from the previous evening and talk a few moments about what is coming up that day at school. Ask pointed questions. Anticipate what might happen. Review upcoming quizzes, events, and assignments with your child, and discuss what needs to be accomplished that day at school. Remind your child about the homework notebook (*more about that later*) and keeping track of assignments. Add a bit of encouragement. Check that everything is complete, packed, and ready to go.

Underlying the daily schedule is the importance of established routines. Disorganized youngsters tend to plan their days haphazardly, if at all. Routines help children remember the things they need to do by turning regular daily tasks into habits. Habits free up the child's mind from having to remember so many specific tasks, and allow kids to be mindful of new information and significant changes in the daily schedule. To help your child remember what to do, to save organizational time, and to free yourself from the drudgery of constant reminders, establish routines for morning, afternoon, homework, and bedtime.

The Backpack: Most parents never realize how important it is for a child to consistently transport every essential book, note, and paper back and forth between school and home. At school, kids often discover that they have left the things that they need at home. At home, they get ready to study and find that the materials they need are still at school. This is such a problem that a few school districts have purchased dual sets of textbooks—one set for each child's home and another set for the classroom, investing over $1,000 *extra per child* to make sure all children always have the materials they need.

I began my teaching career in 1975 in a small Colorado farm town. That first year, I experienced such a dramatic problem with an underachiever that I still remember it vividly, thirty years later:

Gradebusters

✪

When Coralee's mother came into the classroom after school, I knew I was in for a battle. Her daughter had just entered junior high school, and, although she had done well in elementary school, Coralee had received warning notices from three of her new teachers. Her average in my class, about 43 percent, was the lowest of all my students. Her mother was livid. "Coralee has always been an exceptional student, and received several awards in her last school," her mother told me in a very excited voice. "Now, you people tell me she is failing? I don't think you know what you're doing, and I don't think this is a very good school."

She went on to explain that several of her daughter's friends had also received failing notices, that she knew I was a first-year teacher, and that all the children had loved their last teacher at elementary school, where they had been much happier. She angrily declared that she was going to complain to the school board if the quality of teaching at the school didn't improve.

By now, you can probably recognize several errors that Coralee's mother made:

- "Rescuing" her daughter
- Not getting the facts
- Blaming, defending, and over-generalizing about the state of her child's education
- Never getting around to specifically describing the actual problem.

When I examined Coralee's grades, however, I was able to explain to her mother that Coralee had failed to turn in a number of assignments. Later, Coralee brought in the work, along with a note from her mother explaining that they had found it all, complete and in good order, at home in Coralee's room.

The problem had not been academic, but organizational. Coralee had not gotten used to transporting things back and forth to school, a task she had not been forced to deal with in elementary school. Her mother began to help Coralee with her organizational problems, and her grades improved dramatically.

To organize and transport work and supplies between school and home, and vice-verse, your child needs a backpack and an assignment notebook. These are the organizational basics. Make sure that the back-pack is stylish or your teenager won't use it. Buy an assignment note-book that is substantial and durable, not one of the cheap spiral pocket ones. Consider preparing and copying a custom homework sheet to send and review each day that includes a place for teachers to initial and a check-off when work is complete. (*Sample homework sheets are reproduced at the end of this book.*)

Regardless of the circumstances, your child needs to carry the back-pack and the assignment book back and forth to school every single day. This must be an absolute, unvarying routine.

- Pack and unpack the backpack at the same location each day. If you are using a desk, for example, everything should go from the backpack onto the desk, and from the desk back into the backpack. This avoids leaving schoolwork around the house and losing important information and work in the clutter.

- Check the backpack and homework notebook every evening after school in your youngster's presence. Make sure that all assignments are included in the assignment notebook, and that all homework necessities are in the backpack.

- Check the backpack every morning, again in your child's presence. As you do so, go over the day ahead, previewing together how the day will go and what to expect. In schools, teachers call this process—of preparing kids for what is to come—"advanced organizers." What is going to happen in math class? Are you ready for the quiz in reading? Is everything there for social studies today? Be aware that children are notorious for doing their homework and leaving it at home. Remember that even bright kids have problems with organization.

- Keep the bag organized and free of loose paper and trash. This is your child's base of operations while at school. By organizing school materials with your child, you are helping to organize his mind for the school day ahead.

- Review the homework notebook daily. If you can, get the teacher to check it and initial it. Your child should note each subject and assignment, and if there is no homework, write "none." This eliminates later doubt that your child failed to write down the assignment.

- Buy one pencil or pen that is to remain with the backpack at all times and is never to be loaned to another child or used for schoolwork. This is a notebook pen, used *only* to jot down assignments and reminders.

- Stock tissues, hand-wipes, a comb, and other grooming items in the backpack. This will reinforce the notion of the backpack as a single base of operations.

School Supplies: Some kids come to school with so many supplies and novelties that they become hopelessly disorganized. Purchase only those school supplies that the teacher requests in writing, plus an assortment of pencils or pens, depending on what the school requires. (Many schools do not want kids to bring pens to school.)

Buy a 12-inch ruler, a 3-ring binder, and some lined paper, and make sure you always have a stack of notebook paper at home. A glue stick, an eraser, and a zippered pencil case are all cheap and useful. Avoid colored markers, sharp scissors, stickers, indelible markers, "white-out," or bottled glue. Your child should not need a hole punch, fancy or colored paper, journaling books, art supplies, drafting implements, exotic pens or inks, a calligraphy instrument, broad-tipped markers, or other sorts of non-essential supplies.

Don't buy anything fancy or glittery. Middle schools are full of pink and purple pens, glitter glue, day glo markers, and ink stamps. Kids use these items to decorate their papers (instead of working on them), to write to their friends, and to draw with during class.

Many parents, at the urging of their youngsters, buy too many school supplies. These supplies can be expensive (especially if you have several children) and are usually unnecessary. Stick to the basics, and make sure your child has plenty of them. Fancy school supplies will not help your children do well academically, and may actually distract them from important work at school

Computers: Software manufacturers and Internet service providers hail computers as an important aid to self-directed learning, but they are usually used by youngsters for other purposes: gaming, net surfing, chat room corresponding, e-mailing or instant messaging friends, and otherwise entertaining themselves. Parents are in a quandary here—if they allow computer use during study time, will their child use the computer to simply goof off and avoid doing schoolwork? Won't the computer derail study instead of facilitating it? On the other hand, isn't it possible that youngsters may actually need their computers for academic pursuits like researching information or word processing?

The practical solution is to oversee computer time. Consider moving the computer into a more public area so that grown-ups can supervise computer use (computer crime experts recommend this, anyway, to subvert Internet child predators). During study hours, kids should be able to explain *why* they need the computer and *how* they are going to use it.

Frankly, I have not found the Internet particularly useful for children who are doing research unless the user has extensive Internet search skills. Most kids get bogged down in the sheer volume of available information, investing a great deal of time to retrieve a small amount of information of questionable value.

Computer CD encyclopedias, on the other hand, have more utility for most school projects and are quite reasonably priced. These encyclopedias are specifically designed for student use. If you have doubts about your child, computers, and academics, leave the computer off. Your youngster will probably get better grades with the machine off than he or she is getting now with it on.

Television: Americans watch way too much TV. Many American families have acquired a "TV habit." They watch shows throughout the evening, even if no one is particularly interested in the programming. Some families, in fact, have become so unaccustomed to quiet in the home that they cannot imagine an evening without TV. For your child, TV time is wasted time that could be better spent on homework and study.

Here are some hints for managing television time and learning how to turn the TV off:

- Break the TV habit by turning the TV off. If someone is channel surfing, it is a strong indicator that the viewer has no special interest in a specific show.

- Develop a viewing schedule. At the beginning of the week, highlight interesting programs in the viewing guide and watch *only* those shows.

- Allow your children to watch TV only after all schoolwork is done and—here's the key element—after it has been checked.

- Establish a video store budget of, say, two movie rentals per weekend, and stick to it.

- Cut down on the noise in your home. All TVs, stereos, radios, and electronic games not being used should be turned off. Establish a nightly quiet time, starting at 9:00 p.m., and turn everything off then.

- Limit how much time your kids spend in front of the "tubes" (TVs, computers, and electronic games). Two hours a day is plenty.

I have counseled many families to try these steps, and parents have reported to me that being in a quiet home was a surprising shock. It took some families several weeks to get used to living without continual electronic noise in their home.

Gradebusters

Homework: Some parents hesitate to get involved in their child's homework. They worry that helping out is actually "cheating." Other parents may not feel fully competent in a subject area. Parents might be embarrassed by their own lack of education or knowledge. They may not want to come to the rescue of their children, and thus encourage their children's poor homework habits.

⋈

For many years, I worked at an elite preparatory school in Colombia, South America. The school prepared Colombian nationals and students from other countries for placement in America's best colleges and universities. The school's standards were rigid. One expectation was for the parents of each student to meet with teachers at least twice each year. Every year, we had a terrible time trying to get Mr. Mesa to attend the parent-teacher conferences.

Mr. Mesa was a self-made millionaire who had built his fortune by importing used luxury automobiles into the country. He was well-known in the international community for his outgoing personality and generosity, and his children were solid, well-behaved students. It was always a mystery why Mr. Mesa would not come to the parent-teacher conferences.

I finally met Mr. Mesa at the graduation lawn party for his oldest son. He approached me to thank me for all the time I had spent helping his children at school. I asked Mr. Mesa point blank why he had never come to the school to meet his children's teachers. "I grew up in the countryside and went to a government-sponsored public school," he explained. "In our village, classes only went until the sixth grade, and I was a horrible student. I never even finished the local school."

Because Mr. Mesa saw himself as academically incompetent,

he thought he was unable to help his children. He confided to me that he often looked at their work and did not understand much of it. "My children do very well at school," he concluded. "I do not want to come there and interfere. I do not want the teachers to know that I am an uneducated man. No, thank you. I support my children in any way I can, but I am not a person who belongs in a school."

What a tragedy that Mr. Mesa never saw himself as a parent who belonged at school! The notion that parents need to be academically accomplished or intellectually sophisticated to participate in the education of their children is misplaced and damaging. Just the opposite is true. Parents who become interested and involved, and show their interest and involvement, help their children tremendously, regardless of their backgrounds and skills. This particularly applies to homework, in the broadest sense of the word.

Schoolwork is what your children do at home. No one from the school is there to organize your child, get him or her busy, structure his or her time appropriately, and check that his or her work is complete. Your children can learn these skills and apply them on their own, once you have taught them the skills. But, at the beginning, you will need to help establish these vital work habits. Furthermore, all children need supervision to assure that their work gets done and that its quality is consistent.

If your child already knew how to manage time and organize work effectively, you wouldn't be reading this book. So, here are some guidelines for dealing with homework:

- Check the homework notebook daily. Use the notebook to help your child organize his evening's study time and work schedule. Plan the evening's work together. Ask questions. Set priorities.

- Schedule the study session for the same time each day. Pick a time when you can supervise. Homework is best done in the late afternoon or early evening. Privileges like TV and computer time should go into effect only *after* the homework is complete.

- Before beginning, organize the study area so that materials are ready and distractions and interruptions are minimized. Do this together nightly.

- Check to see that the completed homework corresponds to the assignments, and that all assignments are finished. Make sure your child did the right assignment. Along with your child, check each assignment off with a pencil as you put it in the folder.

- Encourage in your children a sense of pride about their schoolwork and their homework. Neatness, appearance, spelling, penmanship, and organization are still important to teachers. Don't let your child convince you otherwise.

- Do not check actual content or correct assignments. It is important that your children do their own work. Your job is to make sure the assignments are done, to check for organizational problems, and to maintain quality control.

- Make sure all homework is together, in order, complete, and ready for school. Put it in a folder near the backpack, clearly labeled with name, subject, and assignment. Teachers review several hundred papers each week. Make sure the teacher can identify your child's assignment at a glance.

- Note and track long-term assignments. Poor learners often avoid work until the last minute, or forget it entirely if it is not due tomorrow. Help your children plan their time and ade-quately prepare for long-term assignments, especially in the upper grades, when kids may be given work that is not due for days or even weeks.

Turning homework in on time, and receiving good grades on such assignments, are two things that will help your child's school perform-ance and grades right now. Teaching and developing responsible plan-ning skills will help your child for years to come, and perhaps an entire lifetime. Youngsters who have the best of intentions may not have the management and organizational skills to cope with the demands of school.

✦

Jack was an advanced placement sophomore who was bright, talented, and articulate. His mother, Elaine, was distressed because, although Jack's classroom grades were good, he seldom completed his out-of-class assignments. Elaine and her husband owned a small real estate agency, and their work kept them at the office until the evening hours. By the time Elaine arrived home, Jack had typically made dinner and left with his friends for the evening, his homework incomplete and forgotten.

Elaine and I devised a plan of action that included a backpack and a daily homework sheet. Jack came directly home from school and called his mother, checking in and explaining what his assign-ments were for the evening. After finishing his work, he laid out his backpack, daily assignment sheet, and completed homework assignments for his mother's later inspection. Before Jack could leave the house with his friends, he was required to again call his mother at work, indicating that all assignments were complete and on the table.

When she arrived home, his mother compared the assignment sheet with the completed homework, checking accuracy, neatness, and completeness. In the morning, Jack and Elaine went over the assignments and packed the backpack together.

After a couple of months of using this system, Jack's grades improved dramatically. Elaine decided that it was no longer necessary for Jack to call her office on a daily basis. He simply left the assignment sheet and his completed work on the table before he went out in the evening. Elaine checked that everything was complete when she got home from work. They continued to look over things together in the morning. Once Jack learned the habit of organizing and completing his assignments, the routine took over and he became quite responsible about managing his schoolwork.

The system Jack and Elaine used was successful because of several key factors:

- Elaine quit nagging and formed a plan of action.

- Eliane focused on responsibility, organization, and time management.

- Elaine devised a system where she helped organizationally, but Jack still did the work. Both relied on the power of routines.

- Jack gained a significant payoff by executing the plan. He was permitted to go out with his friends and manage his own affairs as soon as his work was done.

- Elaine maintained a businesslike supervisory role.

- Elaine allowed Jack to take charge when he was able to handle the responsibility, but she continued to keep an eye on his progress.

Remember that your child could be avoiding homework out of laziness, but the problem may also be organizational. You can help. Kids need assistance with planning routines and managing time. Make sure your child has a system for noting and remembering homework. Check daily to be sure all work gets done and gets to school. Teach the daily routines that help kids to manage their school affairs.

CHAPTER TEN

Forging the Home-School Alliance

Doctrine should be such as should make men in love
with the lesson and not with the teacher.
—Francis Bacon

We have seen that many educators are overwhelmed by their own problems and have little time for your children's. Teachers struggle to maintain a semblance of professionalism and order in the midst of an overwhelming bureaucracy, callous and outraged parents, and class-rooms packed full to the rafters with kids.

Your child's teachers may fully realize that your son or daughter is not doing well in class, but have no idea why, or what to do about it. They might not have the interest or commitment to try a new approach with your youngster. They might just be burned out. No wonder your child has gotten lost in the shuffle!

In my thirty years of working in education, I have seen some pretty bad teachers. If I seem to paint teachers in a negative light, however, I do not mean to. Most teachers I know are talented, caring professionals who know their jobs and do them well. If that is the case, you are prob-ably asking, what is the problem? Why can't this skilled professional teach my child?

As we saw in Chapter 2, part of the problem is systemic. Other problems concern the relationship between the home and the school.

They include the following:

- Teachers are education experts, but they do not know your child intimately.

- You are the expert on your child, but you don't know much about how modern schools work.

- Effective communication between the school and the home seldom takes place.

- There is no continuity between what goes on at school and what happens after your child gets home from school.

- Your child views school and home as two totally different worlds and acts quite differently in each place.

- Your child understands, and can manipulate, the lack of home-school continuity.

- Many teachers are "gun shy" about parents because they have had bad experiences with parents.

- A teacher cannot initiate contact with all parents. There simply are too many of them.

If you are fortunate to have dedicated teachers working with your child, they are probably as fed up as you are, and want, need, and will seek your help, once they sense that you mean business, that you will not criticize and complain, and that you won't waste their time.

It is vital, however, that you understand this—*you* must initiate the contact with the teacher, and *you* must administer the plan. You must portray yourself as a competent parent who is there to help, not as someone asking the teacher to assume additional burdens. You must quickly and efficiently work around the teacher's tight schedule.

If this sounds difficult, remember that the failure to establish effective lines of communication with the teacher may create a great deal of the stress and frustration surrounding your child's education. And, keep in mind that the rewards for beginning a positive working relationship with the classroom teacher are tremendous.

✿

Years ago, I taught at a small Colorado school in a low-income rural area. Sensitive to the income level of the community's parents, the teachers put together a school-wide list of the minimal school supply items parents needed to purchase for their children's schoolwork, and sent the list home with each child during the first week of classes.

In late November, I received a call from a mother who was furious because, as she put it, "I am sick and tired of having to go to the store and buy school stuff for my daughter. Does she really need all this stuff? Do you think we're made of money?"

It seems that the mother had never received the school-wide list of supplies from her daughter, who had been asking her to buy stickers, candy, colored markers, a backpack, and even make-up, because, she said, she "needed them for school." The mother admitted that many of her daughter's "needs" seemed odd, even implausible, but she had not wanted to call the school and "cause a problem."

The parent in this example made several common mistakes. She did not establish early lines of communication. Instead, she waited to call until she was fed up and angry with the school. She hesitated to make contact with the teacher because she did not want to "cause a problem," which itself caused a problem. When she called the school, she complained and attacked the teacher, thereby becoming the stereotypical "problem parent" in the teacher's eyes.

She did not call first to determine the facts. She relied on her child as a messenger instead of using direct communication. Finally, she allowed her daughter to manipulate the situation by playing the trump card, "How can you expect me to do better in school when you won't buy me the stuff I need?"

If this mother had contacted the school earlier in the year, and formed a working alliance with the teacher, things might have been different. A personal relationship would have developed before problems occurred—a relationship built on trust and mutual regard instead of anger and suspicion. There would have been open lines of communication, an assignment book, and contact numbers. The mother would have known what was going on daily at school. And, the daughter would have known that Mom knew.

In addition, the mother would have called the school with her questions *before* the buying spree, not after she had spent money unnecessarily. She would have found out there was a published list of supplies, and gotten a copy directly from the teacher. The mother's lines of communication would have helped her manage her daughter's school affairs, and would have helped the teacher, too. When the mother called, she was already misinformed, furious, and blaming the school— precisely the kind of parental crisis that consumes teachers' time, makes them wary of parents, and drives them nuts!

Keeping in mind that you are the expert on your child, that the teacher could probably use your help, and that forging the alliance is up to you, here are some steps to begin a positive working relationship with the school and your child's teacher:

- Call the school and ask for an appointment with your child's teacher. Set a time limit for the meeting, say, 30 minutes, and arrive promptly. Don't put off making the call.

- Avoid adversarial beginnings. Explain to the teacher that you are not there to criticize or blame anyone. Smile. Be empathetic. Note that you believe the teacher is doing a great job and that you are ready to work with the school to get to the bottom of the problem.

- Explain that you are reading this book and believe in the importance of the home-school alliance. Suggest a partnership.

- Assure the teacher that demands on her time will be minimal and that you will be responsible for the majority of the work.

- Find out the specifics of the problem. Is work missing or of poor quality or both? Does your child seem confused, or just lazy? Get an honest assessment from the teacher. Examine your child's actual work. Take notes.

- Try to avoid jargon. When discussing children, teachers often use a professional vocabulary that most people are unfamiliar with. If you're not sure what the teacher is saying, ask for clarification. Get explanations.

- Try to agree on a plan of action. Take responsibility for administering the plan. Focus on what you can do, but let the teacher suggest what she might do.

- Ask for regular, frequent communication. Get a contact number or e-mail address. Encourage the teacher to call or e-mail before a problem becomes serious. Assure the teacher that you will never take more than a moment of her time.

- Try to begin a personal relationship with the teacher. A teacher-parent relationship will not be as effective as a person-person team. Get on a first name basis with the teacher, and encourage the teacher to call you by your first name. Be open, friendly, and genuine.

- Do not depend on your child to be the messenger. Find a way to communicate directly with the teacher on a regular basis.

- Keep your word. Whenever you communicate with the teacher, be brief, avoid blaming, get to the facts, and jointly agree on a plan of action. If you commit to something, do it.

- Portray yourself as an efficient professional, not a "problem parent."

- Keep taking the initiative. Do not rely on the teacher to maintain the home-school alliance.

- Follow through and keep track of progress. Is the plan working? Have things changed? Is it time to try something else?

Each time you communicate with the school, keep several points in mind. There is no need to be embarrassed or ashamed. You have done nothing wrong. Do not criticize the teacher or blame anyone. This is not a time to bemoan the personality defects of your child or commiserate about his bad grades. Discuss the problem, get specifics, and decide on a plan of action. Focus on what you can do instead of asking the teacher to do more. Follow through. Act efficiently and professionally, remembering that you are the expert on your child.

For a working parent, it may be difficult to arrange a face-to-face meeting with a teacher during the work week. But keep this in mind: You will probably need to meet with the teacher just this once, after which the lines of communication will be established. Then you can exchange information by other means, like telephone or e-mail. Thus, for that critical first meeting, it might be well worth it to take some time off from work. If this is not possible, call the school and request a telephone conference at an arranged time. Avoid simply calling the teacher unannounced, because you may not get his or her full attention then.

Finally, do not let your newfound alliance be a secret. Tell your child of these meetings, conversations, and plans. Each time you talk with the teacher, be sure your youngster hears about your discussion. Tell your child about your concerns and those of the teacher. Lay out the action plan. Stress that lines of frequent communication between the home and the school have been established, and that you and the teacher are now working together on solving the problem.

◇

When There is a Problem

Most relationships you develop with teachers will be positive and productive if you follow the steps outlined above. Sometimes, however, a conscientious parent encounters a classroom or teacher problem that requires intervention from higher-ups. If you feel that you are getting to the point where you want and need to complain, certain steps will ease the process and improve your chances of getting positive results:

- Check out the facts before you complain. Get specifics. Do not rely on your child and his or her friends for information. Children often deliver wrong and biased information.

- Communicate directly with the teacher. Do not use your child as a messenger.

- Tell the teacher your concerns. Be honest and open. Do not accuse or blame anyone. Try not to put the teacher on the defensive. Reaffirm that you support the teacher and think he or she is doing a great job.

- Listen carefully to the teacher's explanation. Do not continue the conversation until you fully understand what the teacher is doing and why. Try your best to understand the teacher's point of view—the teacher's side of the story.

- State your views if you believe that the teacher is wrong. Instead of accusing, explain what you want to have happen. Look for common ground. Never appear to be taking your child's side, even if you are.

- Move quickly from a discussion of the problem to a discussion of the solution. Find common ground and use it to propose a new plan of action. Propose a compromise. Don't try to win. Try to solve the problem and leave the meeting or conversation with a plan of action.

- Never undercut or criticize the teacher in front of your child. At home, praise the teacher. Do not allow your child to talk about the teacher disrespectfully in front of you.

- Avoid school gossip and parent cliques. They are a great source of misinformation. Again, praise the teacher in public and criticize her privately, if at all. Stick to the facts and act like a professional.

- Call the principal if you cannot solve a problem with the teacher. But, make sure you have exhausted your options with the teacher first. Follow the same approach with the principal as you did with the teacher: Don't blame or accuse. State what you want to happen. Try to quickly move beyond discussing the problem to agreeing on a course of action that solves the problem.

It is important to remember that you and the teacher do not need to see eye-to-eye on every detail to get the job done together. But be partners, not antagonists. The teacher is your colleague and ally—be considerate and act professionally towards the teacher.

I sensed that we might have trouble with David from the very beginning. As the leader of a sixth grade teaching team made up of twelve staff members, I was responsible for monitoring the transition of almost two hundred youngsters into middle school. In the fifth grade, students worked in self-contained classrooms with one teacher. In sixth grade, they traveled from room to room, and teacher to teacher. Some students thrived in the new environment. Others seemed lost and confused.

Whatever the reason, David was not making it. Although he had been a strong student in the primary school program, several teachers and aides mentioned to me, within the first month of middle school, that he was quickly falling behind.

I contacted David's mother, Jeannie, and she came to school the very next day. Over coffee in the lounge, I explained my teachers' concerns. Jeannie frowned, nodded her head, and said, "OK. Whatever the problem is, we need to fix it, right now. Just let me know what you want me to do and I'll do it. I know David's father will help, too."

Together, we decided to have a meeting with David and his teachers. At the meeting, Jeannie held David's hand while I out-

lined our concerns. She told David that she was not angry and that he was not in trouble. "I just think you need some help," she gently explained to him. We outlined a plan, including an assignment notebook, a homework binder, and a daily checklist for David to complete. The teachers agreed to tell me at our weekly staff meetings how David was doing and if his work was complete. Each week, Jeannie and I exchanged e-mails about David's progress. She also contacted me via e-mail with any questions and concerns she had about his schoolwork.

At home, Jeannie and David arranged a daily study time immediately after school. There was to be no TV and no video games until his schoolwork was done. As he packed up his work each morning before school, Jeannie checked his work and signed off on a homework form. She also signed his graded papers and returned them to school. When David asked to join the basketball team, we agreed that he could play as long as he maintained his grades. I arranged a reporting system with his coach.

David passed sixth grade with a solid B average. Jeannie asked if I would continue to supervise David in the seventh grade. I agreed, and enlisted the support of his new teachers. We maintained our cooperative parent-teacher relationship until David successfully made the transition to high school. David did not become a truly outstanding student in our middle school, but with organizational help and his mother's supervision, he did well. Perhaps more important, we together built the skills that would allow David to survive in high school, and, we hoped, in life.

I had opened the dialogue between Jeannie and the teachers, and I had proposed the plan. But she took over the initiative and the responsibility, and she deserves the credit for helping David develop the attitudes and organizational skills that made him an academic success story.

Jeannie did everything right—she didn't explode, didn't moan or blame, and didn't punish or threaten. She devised a plan of action and kept on top of it. She worked closely and personally with David's teachers. She operated quietly, efficiently, and with a minimum of fuss. And, she quickly got to the root of David's problem and fixed it.

She and her son succeeded, and so will you and your child, if you forge a home-school alliance. Establish a personal relationship with the teacher. Use it to be aware of what goes on at school, and why. Use it to manage a joint plan of action with your child's teacher. Your child's teacher really does want success—work as a team to make success happen.

CHAPTER ELEVEN

The Social Side of School

I pay the schoolmaster but 'tis the schoolboys that educate my son.
—Ralph Waldo Emerson

Researchers have recently detected an alarming trend among American youth. They are increasingly sedentary and obese. For the first time ever, American kids are more out of shape than their parents. We are raising a generation of youthful couch potatoes. There are several factors that contribute to this unhealthy lifestyle:

- Kids eat less healthy meals and more fast food than ever before. Many schools even house fast food outlets instead of a traditional cafeteria.

- Parents are more fearful of allowing their children to play outside while unsupervised by adults.

- Youngsters increasingly spend their time using computers and electronic video entertainment.

- Children watch an average of four hours of TV *daily.*

Some underachievers, like Marie in Chapter 7, are so busy that academics fall by the wayside. Others (remember Brad, the computer "genius" in Chapter 1?) become socially isolated, physically lethargic, and generally apathetic about school. Both extremes are equally harmful to academic achievement.

Have you paged through a high school yearbook recently? Do you remember yours? It is fascinating to note that the kids who had the highest grades are often those who were most active in extracurricular activities. Whether it is sports or yearbook or debate club or chess club, these students found ways to enjoy the social aspects of school, and their participation in the school culture contributed to their academic success. These kids liked school, liked being at school, and enjoyed the various activities that surround school.

Other kids, however, involve themselves in the social side of school in more negative ways, forming, joining, or becoming part of cliques, gangs, or insider groups. The social elitism that surrounds many high school activities can be destructive to positive attitudes about school. Many kids learn to hate school because of the social cruelty they encounter there.

Many kids feel left out of their school's social world. Sports require a certain degree of strength, coordination, and physical prowess. Tragically, spots on cheerleading squads are often reserved for girls who are attractive and shapely. Many school-sponsored activities are seen as the exclusive turf of elite groups and cliques. Outsiders can be cruelly snubbed—students seen as socially undesirable are sometimes mocked and bullied. Many kids view membership in the socially elite groups as an unreachable goal, and give up trying to compete in what they see as a lose-lose situation.

Less popular kids sense the shallow nature of the social competition that takes place at school, and simply elect to withdraw from all organized activities sponsored by the school. Anger, fear, and resentment are commonplace. Some kids view their chances as better with the other sorts of groups—troublemakers, truants, drug users, gangbangers, and the like.

◆

Eric had always done well in school. Though somewhat isolated socially in elementary school and junior high, he managed to have a few friends and to get good grades. He became involved in Little League and the Boy Scouts. His teachers reported that he was quiet and likeable, and while not a model student, better academically than most.

When Eric entered high school, however, things began to fall apart for him. He became increasingly detached from the social aspects of school. He came home angry and frustrated, complaining that he was often mocked by the popular girls at school and bullied by the "jocks." Pushed around in the halls, he soon allied himself with a group of similar social isolates—kids who wore long black coats, avoided the popular groups, scorned school activities, and projected a tough, angry image. Eric and his friends enjoyed computer simulations and fantasy games that emphasized extreme violence.

Eric's grades dropped, and he became increasingly bitter about school and grades. He believed that teachers, classmates, and school administrators admired and condoned the more popular athletes who bullied and mocked him. He became filled with resentment at the rejection he felt from his classmates.

Eric is not an example from my personal case files. On April 20, 1999, Eric Harris and a friend walked into Columbine High School in Littleton, Colorado, and opened fire on their classmates with semiautomatic weapons. Before they had finished, 13 were dead and 25 injured. Eric came from a stable, middle class family. His parents were supportive and caring. Yet, the social viciousness of his school and the cruelty of his peers turned this disturbed individual into a psychopathic madman.

Most social isolates do not end up like Eric Harris. But it is a sad commentary on the American school system that sports stars and cheerleaders are still held up as model students—instead of socially responsible or academically successful youngsters. Some students simply can't compete, and they are pushed aside and excluded from the school's social mainstream. At an age when social standing, popularity, and romance mean so much, social exclusion can be demoralizing. A miserable social life at school can be academically destructive and emotionally devastating.

As adults, we tend to forget how important the social side of school is to youngsters. School is the hub of a social system that can provide friends, romance, status, prestige, and social standing. We parents view school as an academic institution, but for youngsters, school is the center of their social world. The social side of education can have a tremendous impact on whether your child thrives or barely survives academically. So, remember the principle:

For youngsters, school is very much a social institution.

There are positive ways to become involved in the social side of school, and such involvement does a great deal to promote academic success. Let's note some of the things that are good about school extracurricular activities:

- Kids who are socially involved enjoy going to school and like being there. The school day is not a negative experience—it is something to look forward to, even eagerly so.

- Extracurricular activities are positively organized. They encourage kids to be responsible, to actively participate, and to involve themselves with other students in constructive pursuits.

- Children who are involved in extracurricular activities are involved in the culture of the school. They see the school day as more than work, books, and assignments. They learn that teachers and peers are approachable individuals. Their social world and their academic world are not separate and distinct.

- Extracurricular activities are closely allied with the culture of success. Kids learn about being on time, following directions, teamwork, helping others, working towards common goals, and following through on commitments.

- Participants are treated as important team members. They no longer feel like outsiders at school. They become school participants instead of school spectators.

⬦

Lori was unbearably shy, and she was terrified at the thought of entering a high school of almost 5,000 students. Almost fifteen-years-old, and still skinny and gangly, she was self-conscious about her appearance and her lack of social skills. Lori lived near a school boundary, and most of her friends were going to another, smaller high school. She would be almost alone in a strange and threatening environment.

Lori had played the flute in her junior high school band. Her teacher, Mr. Poblete, called the high school and gave a heads-up to his colleague and friend in the high school band program. On the first day of class, Lori found a note on her locker:

"Hi, Lori. Welcome to Bear Valley High School. I hear you are a fantastic flutist! Please stop by today. I want to meet you. I am in Room 53, the band room. —Mr. Miller

The band gave Lori a sense of belonging, and Mr. Miller quickly facilitated some beginning friendships that soon blossomed into life-long relationships. Lori still felt a bit lost among 5,000 students, but in the band room, she found a sense of belonging and companionship. Band helped her develop a feeling of confidence, and soon she was involved in the school's sports and community events. Lori was no longer an outsider. She felt she belonged at Bear Valley High School.

What wonderful teachers! Mr. Poblete sensed Lori's shyness and made the extra effort to ease her transition into a new school. Mr. Miller took the initiative to seek out this shy girl—one in 5,000—and make her feel at home. Lori's involvement in extracurricular activities facilitated her social and academic success. Membership in the band "greased the wheels" by involving Lori in a positive, productive pursuit. She became involved in the culture of the school—and the culture of success. She blossomed into an important team member. She became more socially comfortable. She enjoyed going to school.

Extracurricular activities were successful in promoting Lori's social involvement. But, school clubs and teams are not always a positive experience for everyone. I've already hinted at some of the more negative aspects of school-sponsored extracurricular activities:

- Extracurricular activities tend to be exclusionary. That means there is an insider group mentality, and outsiders may be unwelcome or snubbed.

- The social cruelty common in many schools can be emotionally devastating.

- Extracurricular activities may require special skills or abilities. Choral groups need people who can sing well. Sports programs need kids who have athletic ability.

- Students can become overly engrossed in extracurricular activities, to the exclusion of other things, including their schoolwork.

There are certain social groups in the school that should be avoided. These groups tend to be anti-establishment and adhere to values contrary to the rules of the school and the goals of education. Groups like gangsters, troublemakers, anti-learning cliques, and school toughs are known as "outsider groups." The outsiders attract kids and have their adherents, too. When the school-sanctioned program is weak, the outsiders gain power and popularity. Paradoxically, "the outsiders" may actually become the insider group of choice at some schools.

The problem is that many kids become involved in these groups because they are the only groups that accept them or offer them a sense of belonging. Some students hang out with the "bad" kids because they think it might enhance their image of being tough or "with it." Youths who have been rejected by the more elitist groups may buy into the culture of negativism that surrounds the outsider groups. Students who resent authority—bullies, delinquents, and those who have a weak sense of self—often end up in outsider groups. Violent and predatory students gravitate to such groups. In one school I evaluated, an outsider group had become so popular and powerful that many students were intentionally failing their classes in order to placate and emulate members of this clique.

Gradebusters

✧

Wellford Junior High School served the small town of Wellford (population 1,200), and the surrounding rural area of about 1,500 square miles. A small school of about 200 students, mostly farm kids, Wellford JHS was locally known for its involved parents. It was the home of the toughest wrestling and football teams in the district. Unfortunately, the school was also home to a small group of ranch boys known as "The Stomps."

The Stomps wore cowboy boots, grippered shirts, baseball caps, and large belts. Around the school, they chewed tobacco, roamed the halls, ditched classes, cheated on tests, and bullied the other students. Avid brawlers, they were often suspended for fist fights on school grounds.

During one school year, several of the school's best students suddenly began to fail classes. The perplexed staff, and several concerned parents, wanted to know what was causing the plunging grades. After a grilling by his parents, one scared boy finally admitted that The Stomps had issued an edict—students who got good grades were "wussies" and would get beaten up. Thoroughly intimidated, many students decided it was easier to fail than to risk the wrath of The Stomps.

This story has a particularly satisfying conclusion—the kind of ending that quickly turns into small-town lore. When the fed-up principal began to call in the parents of the ringleaders, he soon came into contact with the father of Coval Gilbert, The Stomps' chief instigator. Mr. Gilbert, a Korean War Marine, quietly stated, "Well, I'm not surprised my son is involved. But I don't like bullies, and I don't cotton much to troublemakers. Why don't you let me take care of it for you?"

Coval Gilbert came to school the next day and apologized to each of his teachers. No one around town ever heard of "The Stomps" again. Mr. Gilbert never said how he did it, but somehow he put one outsider group out of action, once and for all.

There is another sort of outsider group that has become problematic in certain schools. This sort of group is comprised of computer hackers, Internet surfers, fantasy-game role players, chat room addicts, and video game aficionados. In a strange sort of social isolationism, these youngsters frequently come together to play games, exchange information and expertise (mostly by e-mail), swap website information, and trade programs. But they also avoid the rest of the school's social scene.

The problem is not that these students actively compete against or subvert school values. Instead, they simply cop out of the entire academic process. For many of them, school has become irrelevant to their cyber world, and they choose not to participate in subjects they see as foolish or irrelevant. They don't hate school. They're just not interested in it.

As we've seen, the often overlooked social side of school can be rewarding and motivating. Students who enjoy the social aspects of school generally accept their academic responsibilities more readily. School-sponsored extracurricular activities can have a beneficial effect by teaching social skills, responsibility, teamwork, and proper behavior.

But there can be negative aspects to the social side of schooling. Many of the groups that kids are involved in work against the values of the school. Some disdain schoolwork and academic success. Others are involved in rule violations, inappropriate behavior, violence, bullying, sex, and drugs. Even school-promoted groups can have an elitist, exclusionary mentality. The social world that surrounds the school contains many positive motivational aspects, yet it seems to be easy to run afoul of problems, bad experiences, rejection, and groups of kids who are anything but a positive influence.

◇

Fostering a Positive Social Climate

One of the hard lessons from my own parenting experience is that you can't choose your child's friends. On the other hand, you can provide an environment that lends support to your child's efforts to be socially successful. Guiding your child through the social maze of school requires some insight on your part, and a great deal of patience and understanding. While helping your child become more socially successful, you can introduce your child to the kinds of activities that teach positive habits. But remember that no youngster wants or needs a parent who is trying to be a social secretary!

Begin by knowing your boundaries and adhering to them. One of the most difficult aspects of parenting is allowing your child to develop into a unique individual, even in ways that are quite different from your expectations.

By the same token, you have no business inspecting your child's friends, demanding to know about their parents and families, or asking them pointed questions. Don't criticize friends' dress or tastes unless they are wildly inappropriate. Your children and their friends have the right to their own preferences in clothes, music, mannerisms, and speech habits, even if they seem kooky or strange to you. Remember that good kids come in all sorts of packages.

Don't try to direct your children into the most popular and elitist groups. Let them find their own social niche. Draw the line, however, at promiscuity, criminality, smoking, foul language, immodesty, and anything related to alcohol and drugs.

- Make your home a place that kids want to visit. Be sure your child's friends know that they are always welcome. Try to be hospitable and personable. After all, wouldn't you rather have them in your house than roaming the streets?

- Get to know your child's friends. Introduce yourself. Learn names. Be nice. Don't pry, get nosy, or grill them!

- Remember that your child and his pals do not need another friend—they need a caring, responsible adult who can be a leader in their lives.

- If possible, meet and form alliances with the parents of your children's friends. Call them up and introduce yourself. Unabashedly tell them you believe in forming parent alliances. Call them to check stories, share driving responsibilities, and obtain direct permission for activities at their home that your child has described. Ideally, you should be able to agree on some common rules of behavior (e.g., no drinking, the need for curfews, etc.).

- Insist that whenever anyone is in your house, they follow your rules. Make sure your children understand that this principle applies to their behavior in other parents' homes, too.

There are several things you can do to encourage a beneficial, activity-based social life for your child:

- Insist that your child be involved in some sort of organized activity. School clubs, youth groups, church-sponsored groups, or community organizations might all be appropriate. Allow your children to choose what to do, but insist that they do something.

• Find out, along with your child, what school-sponsored activities are offered. If your child attempts to become involved in one and is snubbed, talk to the teacher sponsor and principal.

• Intervene immediately if your child is bullied at school! You and your child do not have to tolerate bullies. Contact the principal. Insist, in writing, on action and follow-through. If it happens again, call the principal, the police, and the school board. Bullies operate through intimidation. Do not be intimidated.

• Encourage your child to take special classes. Look into martial arts classes, art instruction, computer seminars, crafts lessons, or dancing instruction. Many adult community education courses are also open to children. In our southern California area, martial arts and dancing classes cost about $50.00 a month. The local adult education program offers 10 weeks of painting classes for $77.00.

• Drive your child to activities without complaint. These activities are an important part of your child's education.

• Remember not to live vicariously through your children. Keep your distance and allow them to participate on their own in their own activities. This is the way they learn independence, social skills, and adult responsibilities.

• Do not impose your value judgments on your child's interests. Not everyone is a football player. The important thing is that your youngster is participating in some responsible, organized activity in a meaningful way.

- Take the time to attend when your child is in a play or concert. When they win an award, be sure to show up. Bring the whole family and all the relatives, too. Celebrate success.

Intervening in your child's life does not have to be an entirely negative experience. One of the most important lessons you can teach your child is that strong academics and a robust, enjoyable social life can go hand in hand. Top grades are not exclusively for geeks and bookworms. Many students enjoy good grades *and* an involved social life at the same time.

CHAPTER TWELVE

Off to School

No task is a long one except the task on which one dare not start.
—Charles Baudelaire

ome of you will entirely succeed in changing the academic progress
of your child in just a few weeks. Others may have to wait months for
signs of real progress. The important thing is that you are finally sending
your youngster off to school with all the supervision and organization
you can provide. You have established clear goals, formed a plan of
action to guide their efforts, and arranged consequences to motivate
their performance. You have done all you possibly can to point your
children in the right direction and to spur their progress.

Accomplishing this requires you to move beyond ideas into the
world of action. Many readers of self-help books fail to implement the
ideas the books contain because they forget what they have read or
don't go back through the book and work each step that they have read
about.

Others simply never get around to the hard work of changing the
things that cause discomfort in their lives. The instructional outline
below lists some of the major principles of this book, and my suggested
steps for change. Use it to review your progress, to remind yourself of
some of the key components of the action plan, and to keep track of
strategies you still need to employ.

This book is designed to help you implement a coordinated approach to change. It addresses several related factors influencing school performance. You will have better luck if you apply all of the principles together in a comprehensive way instead of just doing a few things that look promising to you. Review the following "Principles of Action" to remind yourself of the key ideas that form the foundation of the plan. Then, use the Plan Checklist to help you remember the major steps to providing a comprehensive strategy for taking charge.

Principles of Action

Throughout this book, I have mentioned certain principles to keep in mind when beginning a plan of action. These principles will not only help you to focus, but keep you from derailing during your attempts to take charge.

If nothing changes, nothing changes. You can ponder the problem of your child's grades forever, but they won't get any better. You and your child are going to have to do things differently if you want results.

Decide on a course of action and begin today. Don't put it off. You have procrastinated enough. It is time to get busy and fix the problem.

Don't give up before the miracle happens. If you are expecting instant results, forget it. Stick to the program and work for modest gains. Expect resistance. Believe in your child, believe in yourself, and believe in the plan. Things *will* get better.

Teach character. Start early and never give up on this important task. Raising children who have values and are willing to defend them may be your most important parenting task.

The most important attitude to change is yours. Stop being a victim of the bad-grades nonsense. You have waited for others to solve things, to no avail. For your own peace of mind, you have the right to take charge and fix the problem because it is unduly affecting your life.

Don't avoid conflicts—manage them positively. Nurturing, healthy families express attitudes and beliefs honestly and openly. Use conflicts to resolve differences and improve relationships, not to shut down communication.

You are the parent—take charge of your home. Accept your parenting responsibilities and take back the authority you have ceded to the passive-aggressive child who has taken over your home and stolen your peace of mind.

Enforcement must be consistent and unvarying. Like a good cop, avoid emotional clutter and enforce the natural consequences of negative behavior. Your child must learn that negative consequences follow negative behavior like night follows day.

People do things because there is a payoff. Children should gain nothing from earning rotten grades. Make sure there are more consequences than rewards for underachievement.

Punishments punish, but good consequences teach. The most obvious and effective consequences are those that logically follow from behavior. Consequences should make sense.

School is a full-time job. Your child must put school first. As soon as you and your child accept this, decisions about action will become clear.

Decide exactly what you want to have happen. Having vague ideas about what is wrong is of no help. Set goals that explain exactly what you want to happen and when. Make sure they are not subject to interpretation.

For youngsters, school is a social institution. Social success can make school wonderful. Social failure and rejection can turn school into a living hell. Be sure to be a social facilitator.

❖

The Plan Checklist

I have set out a plan of action in considerable detail. If you have decided you are genuinely ready for change, then you are ready to begin. This section is a step-by-step plan of action, as suggested by previous chapters. As you go through the plan, check off each section as you complete it. If you do not remember certain steps, go back through the book and reread the sections that discuss those aspects of the plan. Keep in mind that it is easy to put off the uncomfortable aspects of change.

But, when you find yourself postponing action or waffling about what to do, remind yourself that you are fed up, that you have the right to be done with the bad-grades mess, and that you are committed to action.

Step One: *Make a Decision to Commit*

Before you do anything else, you are going to have to decide to commit to a course of action. Too many parents never get the changes they desire because of their failure to commit. Instead, they complain about their child's behavior, nag, make vague demands, and continue to argue. Decide, once and for all, that you are fed up and that you are going to do this—starting now!

Step Two: *Enlist Support*

You are going to need the help, support, and understanding of your spouse or partner, as well as the other responsible adults around you. Talk to them. Explain your frustration and your plan for implementing changes. Ask for their support and assistance. Try to foster a team mentality.

Step Three: *Confront Your Child*

Do not blame or threaten, but tell your children that their grades must get better. Explain that you will have to fix the problem if your children do not. Offer to provide support, supervision, and help. Mention the home-school alliance—that you and the teacher are in agreement *and* regular communication.

Step Four: *Organize the Home*

Get a homework notebook and a backpack. Establish a study time, as well as morning, evening, and bedtime routines. Check the backpack, homework, and homework book every morning and evening. Organize a quiet study area and remove distractions.

Step Five: *Cement the Home-School Alliance*

Contact the school now. When you meet the teacher, explain your concerns and views. Ask for help. Assure the teacher that you will handle most of the work and not waste the teacher's time. Enlist support, try to agree on a plan, and suggest a homework book that the teacher can initial daily. Establish lines of frequent communication.

Step Six: *Establish Behavioral Objectives*

Make a written list of the things you want to happen. Make the list short and clear. Use language that is not open to interpretation. Describe what your child should actually *do*. Set a timeline. Post the goals in a conspicuous place. Describe the consequences for failing to meet the objectives as well as the rewards for achieving them.

Step Seven: *Work the Grace Period*

Give your child the opportunity to change on his own. Set a timeline—one month, for example—and offer support and encouragement during this time. Emphasize that if your child can handle the problem, you will not have to intervene.

Step Eight: *Monitor Progress*

Throughout the process, monitor progress and maintain frequent contact with the teacher. Review work, look at assignments, and keep track of grades.

Step Nine: *Enforce the Consequences*

After the grace period, review the behavioral objectives. Were they met? If the objectives were not met, apply the consequences. Do not argue or blame. Simply apply the consequences in your role as the supervisor.

Step Ten: *Be a Supervisor*

Do not take your position personally. Like a job supervisor, remember that you are not there to argue or nag. The grades must improve. Either your child can handle it or you will. If your child does not like your methods, he can always take charge himself.

Step Eleven: *Continue to Work the Plan*

Continue with the system of school contacts and consequences. When grades improve, back off and allow your child to be more in charge. When grades begin to slip, take a more active role. Continue to monitor progress via the teacher.

Step Twelve: *Encourage Your Child's Organized Activity*

It is important that your child avoid becoming a couch potato. Encourage an outside interest or class, like art or martial arts, or an extracurricular school activity. Try to direct your child's social energies into positive channels. Get to know your child's acquaintances and their parents. Make your home a welcome haven for your children's friends.

Step Thirteen: *Reward Success*

Be sure to celebrate success. Award progress with increased freedom and privileges. Be a cheerleader.

Step Fourteen: *Build Responsibility*

Continue to stress the natural consequences of your child's behavior. As soon as your children can responsibly manage their own affairs, you will allow them more freedom. When your children can't manage their academic performance, you will have to take over. It is their choice.

If this sounds like a lot of work, do not be discouraged. The rewards for taking charge of your child's education will be bountiful. Academic progress is but one of the success stories you will foster. You will have taught your child important lessons about responsibility, the value of positive social relationships, the rewards of hard work, and the natural consequences of irresponsibility. You may even have shown them the ways they can be effective parents someday.

Most importantly, you will have earned some peace of mind in your own home as you finally end the nightly battles about grades, homework, and school.

Keep in mind that change will be awkward and difficult for you and your child. Demands will be frequent and may seem harsh. No one likes the imposition of limits and restrictions on time and freedom. Be patient and caring. Above all, avoid mixing your supervisory responsibilities with shouting, bitterness, and anger. This is just a job you must do, and the two of you can do it together, cooperatively and productively.

Your child has everything it takes to be a good student. You have everything it takes to be the parent who guides your child to an academically successful future.

You owe it to yourself and your child.

Now is the time to take charge of your child's education.

ELEMENTARY SCHOOL
HOMEWORK SHEET

Date: Day:

Reading

_____Done _____

Math

_____Done _____

Social Studies

_____Done _____

Language Arts

_____Done _____

Science

_____Done _____

Other Work

_____Done _____

All Classwork Done at School?   Yes _____ No _____

Classwork to Finish at Home

_____

_____

_____

_____

Teacher's Initials _____

SECONDARY SCHOOL
HOMEWORK SHEET

Date: _____   Day: _____

Period 1: _____

_____

Teacher Initials: _____

Period 2: _____

_____

Teacher Initials: _____

Period 3: _____

_____

Teacher Initials: _____

Period 4: _____

_____

Teacher Initials: _____

Period 5: _____

_____

Teacher Initials: _____

Period 6: _____

_____

Teacher Initials: _____

Teacher Comments: _____

_____

Reminders: _____

_____

SUMMARY INDEX

CASE STUDIES

Woman who buys self-help books but doesn't use them, 6-7

Super-intelligent computer geek who disdains school, 8

Problem child who thinks she'll become neurosurgeon just because she wants to, 18-19

Drop-out who still expects good job, 19

Capable student who stops trying, 21-23

Teenage girl whose attitudes mirror those of peers, 24-25, 26-27

Teenage girl with exaggerated sense of basketball prowess, 29-30

Bright 4th grader who feels humiliated in front of class, 30-31

Parent who takes child's side about school's emptiness, 31-33

Student who sees school as establishment tool to be resisted, 34

Sister, whose parents praise her for looks, uses comments as excuse at school, 35-36

Juvenile delinquents whose behavior is affected by peers, 38-39

Sullen teenager who shuts parents out of own home, 41-43

Woman who tries to run proper household after divorce, 49-52

Brother who's held responsible for sibling's bad conduct, 52-53

Girl who wants to lose weight but gives up too quickly, 57-58

Author becomes apathetic about college volleyball class, 60-61

Good student who puts social life ahead of main job as student, 61-62

Bright youngster who doesn't see link between hard work and eventual success as rock star, 64

Bright 9th grader who doesn't like school and stops going, 65-66

Author's nephew, branded as "slow learner," improves because of new goal, 67

Parent who disrupts own life to do unappreciated favors for kids, 72-74

16-year-old girl who assumes husband's family will take care of her, 74-75

Teenager who manipulates uncurious, non-confrontational father, 76-77

12-year-old who uses new cell phone without thought to cost, 78-79

Father of wrestler who's too involved in kid's life, 80

Parent who decides to sell home, spend proceeds on gymnastics coach for daughter, 80-81

Mother who encourages son to be Boardwalk scofflaw, 83-84

Parent who backs child/bully at school, 84-85

Conscientious parent who's afraid to mete out punishment to kid, 89

Parent who allows underage child to make too many decisions on own, 92-93

Author's allergies trigger desire to stay home from work, 103

Parents' bribes to thumb-sucking twins don't pay off, 105-106

Missionaries' son forgets that school is his main job, 112-113

Teenager throws eggs at neighbor's pickup truck, pays consequences, 114-116

Teenager plays divorced mother off divorced father, 116-118

Teenager's grades slip because of too much other-than-school activity, 122-123

Teenager fares poorly in morning bedlam at home, 130

Mother who blames teacher for daughter's failing grades, 132-133

Father who cites academic insecurity for non-involvement at school, 138-139

Parent who supervises child's homework despite staying at work in afternoons, 141-142

Teenager who cons mother into buying excessive school supplies, 146-147

6th grader who isn't making it at new, more demanding school, 152-154

High school kid who gets pushed around, tormented by school jocks, 157-158

Shy high school student becomes comfortable because of invited participation in school band, 159-160

Junior high kid leads school gang, until school, father become involved, 162-163

PARENTS

Self-help books and their limitations, iv, 7

Willingness to accept need for change, vi

Why there's no single right way to do the job, vi-vii

Habits and their role in success, vii

Need to ensure own emotional health, vii

Frustration from pushing kids with no school interest, 1

Underachievement as problem for whole family, 2

Going to school and taking child's side vs. teachers/administrators, 4

Feeling powerless in stopping kids' school underperformance, 5

Rationalizing underachievement by saying kids going through a "phase," 4

Need to assume new responsibilities, 5

Factual information remembered or forgotten from own schooling, 10

Increasing inability/unwillingness to help children with class work, homework, 14

Wish for diagnosis of learning disability in children, 23

As early influence on children, 23-24

Declining influence of, 25-26

Enabling children to be apathetic about school, 31

Right and wrong way to approach, deal with teachers, 31-32

Teaching character, values as antidote to student apathy, 38-40

Determining who's the real boss of the family, 41

Fear of angering children, 42

Tendency to blame selves for kids' hostility towards them, 43-44

Capitulating to hostile children, 45-46

Extra fears and pressures caused by divorce, 46

Characteristics of nurturing families, 47-48

Characteristics of dysfunctional families, 47-48

Ignoring kids' misbehavior, 51-52

Need to impose consequences on misbehaving children, 53

Conflicts with children inevitable and beneficial if handled correctly, 54-55

Need to avoid being intimidated by children, 55-56

Need to change comfortable routines, 57

Need for realistic timeline for change, 58

Arguments with children don't solve bad grades mess, 59

Permitting kids to stop going to school, 62

Avoiding confrontation with children, 63

Need to focus on own needs, not child's, 65-66

Tolerating children's bad grades and negative attitudes not part of the job, 65-66

Need to change own attitudes before fixing bad grades problem, 68-69

Thinking job requires sacrifices or martyrdom, 69-70

Readily giving in when kids put up a fuss, 73

How to teach kids to manage their own lives, 77

Thinking financial generosity will be endearing to children, 77-78

Gift-giving as sign of insecurity, 79

Need to respect limits of parent-child relationship, 80-82

Hurting kids by rationalizing unacceptable behavior, 83-84

Need to state children's academic problems, appropriate goals, narrowly and specifically, 86-89

Ability to discipline children, child protection agencies notwithstanding, 90

Legal responsibility for child's conduct at, outside school, 91-92

Rights to impose curfews, study times, etc., 93

Rights to apply physical punishment and discipline, 95-96

Most effective forms of punishment, 96-97

Tendency to go wild when child does something wrong, 97

Need to manage own anger, 98

Need to emphasize consequence for wrongdoing, 98

Using the policeman model when changing bad grades dynamics, 99-101

Need to focus impersonally on issues and consequences, 101

Providing payoff to kids for doing better at school, 102

Danger of bribing kids, 103-105

Distinguishing between rewards and bribes, 106-107

Distinguishing between consequences and punishment, 108

How to confront child about grades, 108-111

Emphasizing to kids that school is their full-time job, 111

Need to allow a grace period in executing grade-improvement plan, 111

Sample script for confronting children about grades mess, 111

Need to impose immediate consequences for poor academic performance, 113

Basic parts of plan to end bad grades mess, 113-114

Determining what's taking time away from children's school work, 119

How to monitor grade improvement process, 123-124

Need to check homework on a daily basis, 124

Tendency towards complacency after grades improve, 124

Need to reorganize the "home front," 126

Need to schedule uninterrupted talk with child about bad grades, 127

Establishing appropriate morning routine with kids, 129

Distinguishing between necessary and unnecessary school supplies, 132-134

Regarding computers as unessential study tool for children, 135-136

Recognizing television as children's biggest time waster, 136-137

Getting kids to break television habit, 136-137

Distinguishing between parental review of homework and parental assistance on homework, 138

Ideal role in checking homework, 139-140

How to best initiate contact with teachers, 144-145, 148

Telling children about contact with teachers, 150

Knowing when to go to school higher-ups when teacher doesn't resolve a problem, 150-152

Reasons for not picking child's friends, 164-165

Ways to encourage kids to have active social life with peers, 165-166, 167-168

How to form alliances with other parents, 165

Checklist for carrying out plan to end bad grades mess, 171-175

SCHOOLS

School administrators blamed by kids for poor grades, 3

Systemic failure seen as cause for poor grades, 4

Overcrowding of schools and impact upon students and parents, 11

Overseen by boards composed of non-educational professionals, 13-14

Time spent on non-educational issues, 14-15

Inability to intervene for underachievers, 15

Adopting a "right to fail" policy, 15

As great socializing agents, 16

Good student behaviors that good schools inculcate, 16

Creating culture of achievement, 17, 18-19

Facilitating early successful years in school, 21

Apathy as result of brutal social life at school, 23-27

High school diploma and its diminishing value, 36-37

Social elitism surrounding some high school activities, 155-156

As places where outsiders are cruelly snubbed, 156-157

Role of extra-curricular activities, 159-161

STUDENTS

General attitude towards school problems and failure, iv-v

Reasons given for lacking interest in school, 1

Blatantly disregarding threats and punishments, 2

Typical excuses given for student underachievement, 2

Checklist for underachievement, 3-4

As truants in rebellion against school, 3

Feigning illness to avoid school, 3

Excuse that everyone in class is getting poor grades, 3

Mystified as to why poor grades being given, 3

Indifference to school and good grades, 3

Twisting bad grade discussions into arguments about harsh, unfair parenting, 3

Poor grades blamed on lack of intelligence, 3

As athletes, 8

As computer geeks, 8-10

As cheerleaders, 8

Attitude problems vs. learning problems, 9

Sense of entitlement, 9

Figuring in culture of achievement, 10-11

Drastic change in values and expectations, 16

When homework first becomes a burden, 19

Influence of peer relationships, 23-26

Need to demonstrate independence during adolescence, 26-27

Pre-cursors of apathy, 28-35

Seeing no payoff from school success, 32-33

Social success without academic success, 33

Social standing in school, 33-35

Anger and rebelliousness when played out as school apathy, 33

Apathy as excuse for abandoning, downplaying studies, 35

Job seen as way to gain status and independence, 37

Imagined rights to absolute privacy in home, 41-42

Use of passive-aggressive strategies against parents, 43-44

Rude and insolent behavior disguised by passive-aggressiveness, 44

Playing one divorced parent off against other, 46

Retaliating when household rules are enforced, 46-47

Passive-aggressive personalities common in dysfunctional families, 47

Alleging parental abuse, 49-50

Setting bad examples for younger siblings, 52

Quitting school early, 55-56

Capability of almost all K-12 students to do well in school, 59

Regarding selves as incompetent students, 60

How perceptions of school inadequacy can be self-fulfilling, 61

Link between self-perceived school academic incompetence and apathy, 61

Typical excuses of those who underachieve at school, 61-62

Seeing selves as "victims" of educational establishment, 62

Tendency of some to insist that teachers entertain them, 62

Slacking off at school because there's no immediate payoff for doing otherwise, 62-64

Inability to defer gratification, 63

Difficulty thinking abstractly and into future, 63

Frequent failure to see link between hard work and success in life, 64

Feeling that world will automatically provide what they want, 64

Tendency to not do what's considered boring or unrewarding, 65-66

Assuming that best-performing students are brightest, 66

Link between good grades and good behavior in elementary school, 66

Wanting to be treated as "responsible adults," but also as helpless children, 73

How "learned helplessness" is successful strategy, 74

Believing they're entitled to "things" because other kids have them, 78

Learning most from observing parents' behavior, 82-83

Legal drop-out age, 91

Tendency to "raise roof" when parents are about to change things in household, 101

Payoffs for not performing well in school, 104

Rooms at home reflect organizational bad habits, 127

Why organization is so important to fixing bad grades, 128

Proper study area and its components, 128

Need for background music while studying, 128

Adhering to study schedule at home, 128-129

Need to take breaks during study periods, 129

Need for specific amount of sleep, 128-129

Establishing proper morning schedule before going to school, 129, 130-131

Reading before bedtime, 129

On benefits of properly using backpacks, 130

On benefits of using a notebook summarizing each day's homework assignments, 133

Benefits of extra-curricular activities, 158-159

TEACHERS

Blamed for kids' poor grades, 2, 3

Preoccupation with students having severest problems, 11

Numerous pressures on, 12-13

One thing they'd teach if they had every student for just one day, 16-17

As early adult influence on kids, 23

ABOUT THE AUTHOR

 During an extremely varied career, Stephen Schmitz, Ph.D., has directed curriculum development projects, substance abuse programs, and social service agencies in the U.S. and abroad. He has also worked as family therapist, parenting coach, case manager, health educator, mental health specialist, and chemical dependency counselor in various clinical and social venues.

He earned his undergraduate degree from Colorado State University, and his master's degree from the University of Colorado. His Ph.D. is from the University of Florida, where he earned several fellowships and the College of Education's prestigious Outstanding Dissertation Award. He was a University of Florida President's Outstanding Student in 1993.

For more than 25 years, he has taught classes at schools such as the University of Florida, Spring International Language Center, the University of Guam, the Micronesian Language Institute, and Colegio Nueva Granada.

In addition, he has trained teachers, nurses, researchers, and social workers around the world. His academic research has appeared in such world-class international journals as *Child Welfare* and *Journal of Education,* as well as popular magazines like *Mothering.* His professional interests include adolescent outreach programs, parenting education, adolescent values, at-risk youth, and teenage chemical dependency.

Gradebusters: How Parents Can End the Bad Grades Battle is his first book. His next book, *Strike Back! How Parents Can Bust the Teen Drug Culture*, will tell parents how to detect and handle their children's problems with drugs and alcohol.

He currently lives with his partner, Patricia Walker, in a tiny loft apartment along the Pacific Coast Highway in Huntington Beach, California.

He is now Executive Director of Shanti Orange County, an agency that provides counseling and social services to individuals with HIV.

Dr. Schmitz is available for talks at schools and before parent-teacher organizations. Those interested should contact him directly at doctorschmitz@yahoo.com.

ABOUT THIS BOOK

A BOOK THAT WILL CHANGE YOUR LIFE ...
AND YOUR CHILDREN'S LIVES

Throughout his long and varied career as an educator, Steve Schmitz has been told one story, and asked one question, more than any other: "My child's in grade trouble at school, Dr. Schmitz, and it's making my life hellish at home. I've tried everything, and nothing works. What do I do now?"

From three decades as a counselor, Schmitz knows that most parents deeply want to help their children at school. But he knows all too well how powerless most parents feel in turning their lackluster learners around.

And he knows, from long experience, how often, and how bitterly, parents clash with their children during "you've got to do better" periods.

To keep household conflict from escalating, and to show concerned parents how to be part of the solution, Schmitz put down in book form all the successful advice he's been dispensing for thirty years. In *Gradebusters: How Parents Can End the Bad Grades Battle,* he shares his practical methods with parents disturbed about their kids' low levels of academic achievement.

From hundreds of real-life cases, Schmitz knows his methods work. "There is a way out of the bad grades mess," he says, "if you're really fed up with excuses, blaming, moping, guilt, and anxiety. And, once you finally admit to yourself that you're sick and tired of rotten grades and ready for a change, substantial progress may be easier than you think. If you're also willing to take certain steps, you can take charge of your child's education, and save your own sanity in the process."

Schmitz offers parents a structure and a formula that allow them to take charge without bullying. He offers parents practical solutions for their children's academic success, even in less than wonderful schools. Step-by-step, he guides parents through the process of forging productive alliances with teachers, recapturing lost opportunities for academic growth, and motivating children to learn. It's a highly readable pre-scription for ensuring school success.

Among other things, *Gradebusters*:

- Shows how parents inadvertently perpetuate their kids' bad grades cycle, and provides a step-by-step guide to breaking it

- Demonstrates why many underachieving children don't know why they're getting bad grades

- Explains how parents should go about discussing grades with their children

- Debunks the myth that grades are purely a reflection of a child's intelligence

- Makes clear that certain skills, like organization, may be the most important, and walks parents through the process of helping their children develop the academic skills that will prove useful for a lifetime after school

- Discusses rules and consequences, and how parents can successfully handle this area in the context of improving grades.

Each child, Schmitz believes, has the potential for academic achievement. Parents, he emphasizes, are the key to unlocking their children's school achievement. Because it patiently, and in plain language, explains how and where to begin, continue, and finish, *Gradebusters* fundamentally empowers parents.

So, if you're a frustrated parent whose children are working below their potential at school, read and apply *Gradebusters*. It will forever change your attitudes about parenting, your beliefs about your role in schooling, and your children's future.